THERE'S A NEW FAMILY IN MY HOUSE

THERE'S A NEW FAMILY IN MY HOUSE!

Blending Stepfamilies Together

Laura Sherman Walters

Harold Shaw Publishers
Wheaton, Illinois

ISBN 0-87788-810-8

Library of Congress Cataloging-in-Publication Data

Walters, Laura Sherman.
　　There's a new family in my house! : blending stepfamilies together / Laura Sherman Walters.
　　　　p.　cm.
　　Includes bibliographical references and index.
　　ISBN 0-87788-810-8
　　1. Stepparents—United States. 2. Stepfamilies—United States—Psychological aspects. I. Title.
　　HQ759.92.W36 1993
　　306.874—dc20   92-43627
                                                                                 CIP

99　98　97　96　95　94　93

10　9　8　7　6　5　4　3　2　1

To Tom—My husband, best friend, and family

Contents

Acknowledgments

Just as we do not exist without our families, this book would not have been born without the support, love, prayers, and labor of many people.

Gratitude and thanks to:

Ruth and Jim Nyquist, for their encouragement to undertake the project and the immense amount of time spent on the early versions of the book.

John Hofstra, for his ongoing guidance and support. Without his insight, such a work would not have been possible.

Jonathan Lewis, my wise consultant for many years and trusted colleague. Through the process, he read and reread the book into existence.

Francis Schaeffer, for his body of work both at L'Abri Fellowship and his writings. His acceptance of any questions led me to faith.

Bill Leslie, my spiritual director, previous to the book, who allowed me to find my spiritual path and journey.

A dear friend, who wishes to remain anonymous, for the tireless work in editing and such attention to grammatical detail.

My clients, whose trust and courage have taught me that life and families are really about our own search to find meaning in our lives.

Editor Ramona Tucker, for her patience and encouragement, and to Harold Shaw Publishers.

My close friends Pat Buckley and Doris Bauer, for their support and prayers, always believing in me and urging me to reach a bit farther to accomplish my goals.

My parents, Kay and Bill, who have hung in there with me through all my escapades.

Tom, my husband and love, who finally made me computer friendly. His uncomplaining sacrifices of time, computer work, cooking meals, and giving up weekends to the book for a year, have made it possible to bring the project in on time.

Laura Sherman Walters
September 1992

Introduction

It was a rainy Tuesday morning. Two bewildered parents and three hostile children entered my office, wondering if there was anything that could help their family. The parents, Sue and Dave, had married a year before with their children's approval. Sue had two children: Al, age ten, and Dawn, age twelve. Dave had a fifteen-year-old son, Tim. Sue's husband had died five years earlier, and Dave's wife had left the family and filed for divorce three years before Dave married Sue.

As everyone moved into a new house they had great hopes and dreams for their new family. Sue and Dave talked extensively with their children about the upcoming marriage and felt they had good communication between all the members of the prospective family.

Why, then, was this family sitting in my office looking so discouraged? Soon after the family moved in together the conflicts began. There were fights about who would have which room and about every rule Sue and Dave tried to establish. Battle lines were drawn according to whose family the person belonged to. The children were always shouting: "You're NOT in my family!" or "I wish I wasn't in this family!" The conflict left Sue and Dave at their wits' end, wondering what had happened to their dream family.

Does any of this sound familiar? Men and women with children have more to think about than pre-wedding jitters when they decide to remarry. After all, there are many more people involved in a blended family than just the two spouses who exchange wedding vows.

What Do We Need to Know?

This book is designed to be a road map to the inner workings of the blended family.

First, we'll explore exactly what a blended family is. How do you, as a blended family, want to define yourselves?

Second, family members move into the household with many background problems or "issues." As we uncover what these problems are and learn how to recognize them, your blended family will begin to move beyond mere reactions to symptoms and toward a healthier life together and better communication.

Third, the greatest emphasis in this book will be on helping *all* family members bond together with love and commitment. We'll take a close look at intimacy and what it means.

Fourth, a chapter will be devoted to understanding and knowing your children and how they see the blended family. We'll explore the feelings of separation and loss that all the members of the family experience that prevent the bonding process. We'll discuss non-custodial and ex-spouse problems.

Fifth, we'll address the practical issues of setting up your new family. How can you deal with the conflicts you face? What resources can you make use of?

Sixth, knowing when to seek help for family members, as well as spiritual assistance, is important to your developing family. We'll explore developing a spiritual journey for each member of the family and how forgiveness can bring healing and restoration.

Finally, I'll give you some exercises to try yourself and with your family. These will give you some experience in bringing family members together and will help each of you learn how to talk and really listen to one another.

Why Should You Read This Book or Others like It?

If you are a member of a blended family, you are not alone. With half the marriages in the last several years ending in divorce, many families are starting anew.

The members of your family need comfort and healing from the pain they have experienced in previous families. And all of you will have to cope with family members who don't live with you.

If you are to deal effectively with your new family, you need to consider "the whole person." What does this mean? Each individual's personality consists of the intellect, emotions, physical being, and spiritual being. If the family is to work smoothly, each person must have those parts of his or her personality in balance. This is a tall order for all of us—something that takes a lifetime of work. But the more we read, pray, and interact with others, the more we can develop as individuals and as families.

Let Me Introduce Myself

During my ten years as a practicing psychotherapist, I have had the opportunity to talk to numerous families in different stages of the blending process. In addition, my work with children has exposed me to the loss and grief that family members go through in losing one family and joining another. Each of us struggles to be a part of meaningful family relationships and to work through past pain that intrudes on our present life experience.

In previous years, many of the more conservative churches have been reticent to accept remarriage or to perform marriages for previously married people. This book is not a theological commentary on remarriage; however, members of the blended family need a place to worship and pursue their spiritual journey.

My spiritual journey was born at L'Abri Fellowship in Switzerland with Dr. Francis Schaeffer in the 1970s. There I learned of a personal, unconditionally loving God, with whom we can have any discussion.

Hopes for the Reader

In reading this book, I hope that you will see life as a journey. From birth to death, we are in the process of becoming who we are, as well as who we wish to be. We influence many people positively and negatively along the way. The goal of this book is to help each family and the individuals in it come to know themselves and their inner persons more fully. As you realize how much God loves each member of your family, you can bond with each other in a meaningful and more joyful way.

I do not believe any one book can change your life or give you all the answers. I do hope, however, you may gain some support and insight from reading these pages—and that with the help of your family, and God's guidance, you will find the strength necessary to make changes you wish to make.

1

What Should We Call Ourselves?

Definitions and Tools for Family Building

"I don't have a family," said a little girl sadly, when I asked her to draw a picture of her family for me.

A stepmother cried softly in my office while her husband told of their problems with his son's delinquent behavior since he had come to live with them.

A little boy was so tired from his three-day visitation at his noncustodial parents' house each week that he kept falling asleep in school and was unable to finish his homework at night.

What is happening in so many American families today? The problems that plague households of the 90s are not quite the same as those of earlier decades, yet are more pervasive. Much of the family turmoil is not so easy to grapple with.

The fact is that a large number of people are experiencing a new type of family—*a blended family.*

We can define the blended family as one whose members are brought together not only by birth, but also by remarriage. The definition must be broad enough to include everyone— members who visit during summer vacations, weekends, and holidays, as well as those living in the same place together.

We could also say that a blended family is one that must begin the process of becoming a family after the husband and wife have said, "I do." In a blended family, the marriage comes complete with children. That family faces the task of bringing each member into the family circle.

Who Belongs to Your Blended Family?

Who are the members of your blended family? Obviously, the people who actually live in the same dwelling together. But you must also include the children who *do not* live with you as part of your family, as well as the noncustodial parents who must be visited every week or year or vacation. Even the parents (absent ex-spouses) that you or your children have not seen are silent members of your family. Stepchildren, biological children, stepsiblings and half-siblings, ex-spouses, custodial and noncustodial parents are all part of the picture.

We often associate "blended families" with divorce, but there are other family configurations that suffer the same traumas and adjustments as families of divorce. Parents, children, and siblings who have died still affect the family that remains and are therefore a part of your present family to a certain extent. One teenager was brokenhearted because her father was dying. "He will be gone forever!" she sobbed. I tried to help her realize that her memories of him would be with her forever. Even though the loss of his presence and influence were painful, he had shaped her personality and given her strength to draw from. In dealing with death and separation, families must learn how to restructure themselves. And when the survivors of the deceased join forces with new spouses, siblings, and children, the transition can be difficult and lengthy.

You don't have to have a degree in psychology to realize that with so many people from different backgrounds merging into one home there will be major problems. One stepmother likened the mood swings in her family to the experience of a flying trapeze. "How do you know what problem you are dealing with or what to expect next?" she asked in frustration.

Where Do We Begin?

When a person is about to embark on a new season of life, such as marriage or parenthood, he or she spends a lot of time fantasizing about what that life will be like. The emotions go from excited and joyful to anxious and depressed. Fears come knocking at the door—fear of failure, fear that love will be rejected or not returned. At the same time the imagination glows with visions of love, warmth, and security.

With this mix of emotions and new family members, how should your family set about accomplishing the goal of building a new family?

■ *The blueprint—envisioning your future*

Create an image in your mind of what would be the ideal home environment for you. Draw a picture of it. Can you see it? Close your eyes and give yourself some quiet time to visualize it. You can't put into practice what you can't see. In my work with children, I sometimes ask them to draw pictures of what they wish their family would be like. Children are usually very resourceful at coming up with ideas that could work.

Share your thoughts with your spouse and find out what he or she envisions for the family. Then start to compile a list of qualities that characterize your family. Ask for the children's help with the project, and gather together to discuss how you might put some of the ideas into practice.

Envisioning should be done at least once a month within the first two years of the new family's life together. That, by the way, is about how long it may take to become accustomed to the new family and each person's idiosyncrasies. Situations don't improve overnight after years in the making, so everyone must be given time to iron things out. Each family has its own pace of change.

One family envisioned themselves in a unique way—by making a mural. They got a roll of brown mailing paper and spread it out on the living-room floor; then, using crayons and markers, each drew what he or she wanted the family to be like. The father drew a work space in the garage where he could go to be alone and relax. The mother drew a neat kitchen with flowers and music playing, where the children could join her for cozy talks. One of the daughters drew her bedroom full of stuffed animals and a secret door allowing her access to her parents' room in case she became frightened or disoriented. The teenage son drew a shed in back of the house that would serve as his private sanctum. He drew exclusively in black, yet included all his possessions and memories, right down to the sidewalk leading to the house.

What do you suppose this family learned about each other from these drawings?

The parents learned that their daughter was still afraid the new family would not last. She had some painful memories from the previous marriage and the single-parent household. The son wanted to be independent but still felt anger and sadness over the changes that had occurred in his young life. He needed some privacy to work things out, yet he was not as belligerent as he would have liked people to believe. He really did want to find a way to be part of the family.

The children learned that their parents have feelings and needs, too, and could have their own space without rejecting or abandoning the children. They saw their father's need for creativity and privacy and realized that he would not be as irritable with them if he could have some time alone. They saw their mother's appreciation for beauty and the comfort it would give her. They realized she wanted them to feel nurtured, welcomed, and cared for—that a feeling of security and family unity was important to her.

Since these family members had never lived together before, they needed ways to relate to each other, explore each other's backgrounds, and build relationships that would work for their new family. They put the mural up in the family room to remind them of what each person needed and wanted. Because they had worked together on the mural, everyone was being heard and recognized as a significant part of the family. In repeating this procedure more than once over a period of time, they were able to see how the needs of their family changed.

How do you envision your family?

What are the special needs of each member?

■ *The labor—teaching yourselves and one another*
We learn how to grow and make transitions by looking inside ourselves, gaining input from others, reading, praying, and writing a journal. These are some of the activities that can bring insights and give us knowledge of our inner lives.

I have been writing a journal for years on a variety of subjects. If I'm upset about something and can't identify what is bothering me, I sit down with my journal. As I write, feelings come to the surface and there, before my eyes, is the problem. I can then begin to deal more effectively with what I know is going on, instead of trying to guess or just push down the feelings to try to make myself feel better. At other times, I will stop to do some relaxation exercises or spend time in prayer and meditation.

Family members, especially children, learn best by what they see adults doing and not always by what we tell them. If you, as the parents, are working out your own issues and developing your inner lives, then you will be better able to impart these truths to your family and bring a measure of consistency into their lives. The more we learn about ourselves and who we are, the more we can teach our children to respect themselves and feel confident in developing who they are.

One little girl missed her absent father, of whom she remembered little. She felt angry at her mother for making him go away. The mother acknowledged how sad she must be and reassured her that her father's leaving had nothing to do with her. The mother was honest with her daughter, telling her that the father had been violent and that it was not safe to have him in the house. She gave the child photographs of her father so she would have something tangible to hold on to. She also encouraged the child to draw pictures of what she wished her relationship with her father could be like and talked about other ways of comforting her. The child came up with several ideas. When she felt especially sad she would sleep with the father's picture by her bed or visit her beloved grandfather, who acted as a male role model for her. The mother had worked through the painful memories of her husband's abuse enough that she could provide her daughter with the truth, while recognizing her needs and helping her deal with her loss.

■ *The foundation—supporting one another*

One of the purposes of a family is to lend acceptance when those outside the circle don't. The beginning of the new family is a most crucial time, with every member feeling very vulnerable. Therefore, it is important to focus on how to support one another. Unconditional love and acceptance should be a part of any healthy family, but they are especially needed in the growing-together process of a blended family.

What is support, and how do you show it to family members who are doing something of which you disapprove? Support does *not* mean approval of negative behavior; it means trying to understand that behavior and its motivations. Acceptance may be another way of describing support. Sometimes we can become so focused on behavior—especially in children—that we often lose track of the person, thereby propagating the very behavior we wish to correct. Support means that we are not alone in the struggle but have someone who believes in us and will hang in there for the duration.

A teenage boy was very belligerent with his stepfather. He would not talk to him, left the room whenever he entered, rolled his eyes whenever he spoke, and exhibited generally negative behavior. The stepfather interpreted this as hatred on the boy's part and a wish that the father would leave the family. His first assumption was incorrect; the boy did not hate him, but he did wish that his biological father could be there for him. When the stepfather realized that the child's behavior was not personal but represented his grieving for his father, he was better able to support the boy and defuse the power struggle that was going on between them.

Why is it the parents' responsibility to support the child? Because they are the parents! *The parents' job is to help and support the children and not the other way around!* Certainly, children need to learn to be respectful, caring, and supportive, but they learn these attitudes from adults and then reflect them in their own behavior.

Develop a support group of friends, relatives, and professionals whom you can call upon in time of need. Another person's objective views can be most helpful. Choose those who understand the trials and tribulations of blended families and accept you without judgment or criticism. It helps sometimes to share ideas and vent frustrations with other parents who are in similar situations. Encouragement should be a major part of your support system. So should time away—as parents, you need to feel that you can take time off to relax and get away from family problems.

Becoming a family is a long process, and it takes its toll on self-esteem. We all need understanding, affirmation, encouragement, and advice during the process.

■ *The finer touches—understanding the motivation behind actions*

Family members sometimes have difficulty sharing their feelings with each other. Individuals often talk or act in a sort of private code without realizing what they sound like and look like to other members of the family. Sometimes children are even less able to translate their emotions into words. "We didn't talk about feelings in our family" is a phrase that crops up regularly in my therapy sessions. Being out of touch with these feelings sabotages the process of becoming a new family.

You can find out what people in your family are feeling by interpreting their words and behavior. *Interpreting* is simply trying to figure out what a person is communicating to you, either verbally or through his or her behavior. The simplest way to know what a person means is to ask—although sometimes it's necessary to rephrase the question once or twice in order to get the real answer. The person—adult *or* child—is ultimately the expert on his or her own feelings.

A mother of a first-grade boy could not understand why her son would come home from school every day and throw temper tantrums. She said that his behavior in school was good and, other than the tantrums at home, he seemed fine.

When asked what other changes had gone on in the home in the last year, she stated that she had recently remarried, and the family had moved into a new house. Prior to her remarriage, she and her son had lived on their own in a small apartment. When she asked her son if he was feeling overwhelmed by all the changes in his life, he sobbed and said that he couldn't sit still in school all day because it made him tired. She asked him if he felt that everything in his life had changed too fast, and he nodded. They decided that, in order to help him feel more secure, she would pick him up from school for several weeks, instead of having him take the long bus ride home. After school she provided a special quiet time that comforted him. He could rest, they could read a story, and he could tell her about his day. This worked very well, and before long he was eager to ride the bus with his new friends. He tested his mom a bit, to see if he could get her to pick him up again, but his mother reminded him that their agreement had been to help him deal with his feelings and was not to be taken advantage of. He sheepishly agreed.

This mother interpreted her child's behavior and then supported him as he worked through his feelings of confusion and displacement in the new family. By developing some support and knowing what his behavior meant, she was able to help her son become more accustomed to school. Had she reacted to his negative behavior in a punitive manner, he might not have adjusted as well as he did. His feelings of displacement might also have affected his school performance.

The same principle applies to the adult members of the family. If we can learn to interpret our own behavior, we will be better able to empathize with the other members of our household and lend them the support they need.

Interpretation is not the same as mind reading, which is merely one person's version of what another is feeling. The person whose feelings are in question must be asked for clarification before a proper interpretation can be made.

Interpreting helps because other members of the family feel more accepted and understood. In addition, the real issues that stand in the way of growing together are revealed. The people involved can then decide as a family how to work through their problems.

■ *The maintenance—finding and using spiritual resources*

In chapter 9 we will consider in greater depth the role that spiritual assistance plays in bringing about healing and restoration. Often we need strengths beyond our own in order to put our families back together. Many of us believe that God created families to help us develop and grow in a secure environment and provide us with a frame of reference. Frequently in Scripture our relationship to God is likened to that of a child to a parent. If we have not had a positive relationship with our parents, it is difficult to perceive God as loving and caring, let alone someone who wants to give us guidance and assistance. If we feel that God is condemning us for creating this new family, we will have trouble sticking with the process of bringing the family together.

For these reasons, as well as many others, we need to deal with—and not ignore—spiritual matters. We also need to teach our children that there is wisdom greater than any human insight available to help us. It is important to point out that God loves us unconditionally and is there to be called on when we need help. Children need to understand that God is not a Santa in the sky, but a real spiritual, personal Being with whom we can have a relationship through prayer. It can be frightening to feel that things in the family are out of control. Knowing that God is greater than we are can reassure children and help them begin their own spiritual journeys.

Why are spiritual issues important in the blended family? *Many of the needs we express in our families are reflections of our spiritual needs.* As we seek human companionship within the context of the earthly family, so do we long for a "spiritual bonding" with God our Creator and the larger universe created for us. We seek the ultimate belonging. Our connection with God provides us with the greatest strength and resource possible to help us incorporate our new human family.

Pre-family Therapy

Often, if things have not worked out for us in the past, we wish to "do it right the next time." This is a laudable goal, but it must be approached with realistic expectations before efforts toward it can be successful.

Couples frequently get married without realizing the enormous task involved in the blending of a family. Families anticipating such a union might find professional counseling helpful in dealing with unforeseen problems. The process may help you envision and plan the family life you would like to have. Therapy allows input from all family members and aids them in sorting out what is realistic and what is not. Many churches will not marry a couple unless they go through premarital counseling. If counseling is that important for two adults, how much more important for an entire family? When you consider that many children enter new families not long after the breakup of their original families, then the need for some kind of guidance during this transition seems to be not only a logical step but a necessary one.

More is said about what to look for in a therapeutic setting in chapter 8.

Let me define the term, *therapy,* here, and why we use it throughout the book. *Therapy* is actually the correct term for seeking psychological help from a professional person, such as a psychiatrist, psychologist, social worker, or psychotherapist.

Counseling, on the other hand, refers to the giving of advice or guidance for everyday life. Such services may be performed by career or guidance counselors, to name a few.

A Family Inventory

If you do participate in family therapy, each family member will begin to understand what other family members are thinking and feeling. This can be confusing and painful—it takes a lot of time—but before you can begin to build your family life, you must know what is really going on. What are each individual's problems? What causes anxiety for the children? The parents? What are each of you feeling? If you don't deal with these fundamental questions, both children and parents will have trouble coming together as a family.

This process of understanding one another—of "taking inventory"—must happen whether the family receives professional help or not. Eventually you will have to understand one another, or important needs in each of you will be neglected and grow into bigger needs. This aspect of family building is so important that it is covered in greater detail in chapter 2.

2
What's the Problem, Anyway?

The Eleven Most Common Issues
in the Blended Family

Andy and Ruth met through a mutual friend. Each had been married previously, Ruth once and Andy twice, and each had children by their previous marriages. As single parents, each had had a child living at home for the past year. Andy also had a teenage son who was living with his former wife and giving her a lot of trouble. After dating for several months, Andy and Ruth discovered they had a lot in common and were in love. They decided to get married, and Andy's seven-year-old son and Ruth's three-year-old daughter came with the marriage vows. Andy remained in contact with his first wife regarding the care of their troubled teenage son. Andy's seven-year-old son, Andy Jr., was the product of his second marriage, which ended with the death of Andy's wife when the little boy was five. Prior to the remarriage, Andy Jr. had lived with Andy and was cared for by his paternal grandmother when Andy was at work.

Ruth and her daughter Amy had lived alone together since Amy's birth. Ruth's alcoholic husband deserted the family before Amy was born, and both of Ruth's parents were deceased.

Ruth, Andy, and the children moved in together after the marriage with great expectations that they would live happily ever after. At first things went well, but soon Andy Jr. became disrespectful to Ruth. She had difficulty managing him, espe-

13

cially when Andy was away on business trips. Shortly after the marriage, Ruth discovered to her surprise that she was pregnant. Again, expectations ran high that the new baby might restore family harmony.

Things became more complicated when Andy's first wife called to say she was going crazy with their fifteen-year-old son, Steve. She wanted the boy to come live with Andy for the summer, and Andy agreed without consulting Ruth. Ruth was shocked and overwhelmed but tried to comply for Andy. After all, it would only be for the summer.

Steve arrived two weeks later, and the basement sleeping quarters he was given did not meet with his approval. He and Ruth clashed from the start, and he and Andy did not get along much better. He scared Amy and fought with Andy Jr. Amy began wetting her bed and became weepy, clinging to her mother much of the time. At their wits' end, Ruth and Andy sought help from the pastor of their church.

They were encouraged to come to church more often, hold regular family devotions, and pray for God's help with their family. The pastor told them that divorce was a sin that should not be repeated again. Feeling guilty, and resolving to try harder, they implemented the pastor's instructions. Finally, when Steve stole money from the household account and damaged property in the house, Ruth insisted that they go for counseling. ■

What are the problems in Ruth and Andy's blended family?

What do you think each of them are feeling and experiencing?

> What similar traits do you see within *your* family?
>
> The children's behavior is a certain manifestation of the growing tension. But what is really going on?

Issues are problems that a family has, as a unit or individually. Issues go deeper than the external problems and are usually related to previous experiences and traumas. Following are eleven issues that come up regularly in blended families.

Stereotypes —

Society sometimes tries to assign the role of what your family "should" be like. These ideas can come more specifically from the church or other family members. The family can then take up those stereotypes and try to live up to them.

Ruth and Andy's family really thought they could live the television sitcom dream. They let their fantasy wish control their actual behaviors and expectations. In addition, there was a negative stereotype of the wicked stepmother. Andy Jr. perceived Ruth as someone who was making life difficult for him, especially while his father was away. For years, the negative image of stepmothers has made relationships in the blended family more difficult.

Ruth and Andy's minister also prejudged them by the legalistic framework of his church. He gave them pat answers, rather than perceiving them as real people with specific needs.

■ *Belonging/Uprootedness*

Each person in the story has experienced the loss of the family he or she belonged to and has been uprooted from the place in which he or she originally lived. Each child lived in at least two, if not three, homes. Their original homes, which broke up, were followed by single-parent homes, and then the blended family was formed. No wonder there are behavior problems! Children express their feelings of fear and displacement through their behavior. They need time and reassurance when the family they belonged to has broken apart and a new family has taken its place.

Little Amy felt uprooted and threatened by being in a different house with a different room and two new brothers. Her mother was not as available to her because another baby was on the way. In an effort to obtain comfort and solace, she regressed into infantile behavior.

■ *Trust*

Children believe the family they are born into is permanent, and that family is their entire frame of reference. When the family breaks apart they have difficulty believing in the security of their world. They usually end up living with one parent until he or she remarries. The new marriage brings a secondary breakdown of their trust (e.g., they believed that the single parent would not abandon them for another adult). It is also hard for them to place any faith in the dependability of the stepparent.

The teenager, Steve, had trouble trusting any adults in his life. He demonstrated this through his immense anger at not being accepted by either of his natural parents.

■ *Lack of a shared history*

When individuals of a blended family come together they have not had the same backgrounds. Even if the children have the same parents, they have not shared the same past. Each individual's past experience must be considered, and he or she must be helped through past problems before a total commitment can be made to the new family. Children have a particular need for parental assistance in working through their pain from previous families.

Even though Andy had two sons, they did not have the same backgrounds. They had many issues to work through; Andy Jr. benefitted from a living arrangement with his father that Steve did not share. This affected Steve's relationship with his father and brother. Andy Jr. was still grieving over the loss of his mother and felt abandoned whenever his father traveled. Losing his grandmother as his primary caretaker made the loss threefold for him.

■ Control

When most families come together they have not been able to set down all of the rules and regulations, let alone the more complex roles and emotional ties. A power struggle develops over who will be in charge and what roles will be played within the family. Each member vies for his or her own space and the role that may be the most familiar. The new step-parent goes through special testing with regard to his or her role in the family.

Andy Jr.'s disrespect of Ruth, especially when his father was away, was an example of testing the limits to see how far he could push before Ruth would set limits for him. He was perceptive enough to see that this was an area of weakness for Ruth, since it was something she and Amy had not had to deal with that much.

■ Permanency

How long will this family last? This is an unspoken and fearful question asked by most members of a blended family at one time or another. This question most particularly pops up when conflicts and stresses arise. Parents tend to fear failure when their children are unhappy and act out their frustrations. They wonder how long they will be able to live with the tension.

Steve's situation is the most obvious; his living situation is temporary, and his feeling of not being wanted is strong. This sets off a chain reaction in the other children; will they be sent away if they are bad? Additionally, they wonder, *What is this bully doing in our house?*

■ *Lack of preparation*

What is it like to live in a blended family? Many people are ashamed to talk about their experiences and try to hide the fact that they are not with their original family. These secrets and the accompanying myths may be as damaging as any behavior that goes on in the blended family. However, families are usually so busy with the nuptial plans and the living arrangements, not to mention the financial strain, that preparation for the emotions and reactions of each person gets lost in the fray. Some premarital counselors and pastors understand the dynamics of blended families, and there are some support groups that would be helpful.

Andy and Ruth's pastor was not trained in the complex problems of blended families. Many well-meaning people give standard answers, thinking all families are the same. Knowledge of what blended families must go through—both emotionally and spiritually—to bring healing and restoration to their families is crucial. Couples must work on combining their parenting skills and becoming aware of the special problems involving the blended family—long before the marriage takes place.

■ *Guilt*

Parents in blended families may feel a tremendous amount of guilt, particularly if they are the ones who left the first marriage and children from that union. Some parents also feel guilty that in choosing to have another adult companion they have put their own needs before those of their children, especially if the children voice their disapproval of the new spouse.

Children often feel guilty for their parents' breakup and blame themselves. Then when there is conflict in the new family, their guilt is compounded and they feel that they are once again to blame.

Each member of this family seems to be having his or her own version of guilt. Andy feels bad about having neglected Steve, thus deciding to take him into the home without discussing his decision with Ruth and the children. Andy Jr. is feeling responsible for his mother's death and thus gives Ruth a difficult time. Steve believes he should have tried harder to get his parents back together, resulting in his attempt to get them to communicate through his negative behavior. Ruth thinks that if she were just a better wife, mother, and Christian, she could help Andy Jr. and Steve. Amy, too, believes that if she had been "better" her mother might not have married into this horrible family!

■ *Boundaries*

All of us need our own space, and some people need more than others. Boundaries really have to do with feeling safe—knowing that when you say "no" to another person, they will respect that limit and stop the intrusion. This could be as simple as respecting another's desire for privacy in his or her room or not teasing a younger stepsibling.

The issues involving boundaries overlap with feelings of belonging and control. Each person in the family needs his or her own room or space, as well as the sure knowledge that his property is protected and he is in no danger of being harmed. In addition, each family member needs to know that he or she will be safe from name-calling and ridicule, especially with regard to those weaknesses that we all have, weaknesses that are easily revealed in the intimate contact of daily family life. Boundaries have already been broken through death and divorce. Children do not choose where they will ultimately live; adults make those choices. Therefore, the boundaries must be reconstructed carefully and with the consent of the governed, so to speak. Each member of the family should be consulted as to what boundaries will allow him or her to feel safe.

Steve's behavior offers us a clear picture of boundaries gone awry. Apparently he had pushed his mother's limits to the breaking point. He had nothing to protect him when he came to live with Andy and Ruth, having neither a permanent home nor a satisfactory room of his own. When he observed no boundaries of respect, either with the other children or with Ruth, he made the family feel as unsafe as he felt himself.

When one member of a family is intrusive, often it is because he is feeling intruded upon himself. Talking with the intruder to see if this is so can help resolve the problem.

■ Religion

Organized religion can be helpful or harmful, depending on how it is used or misused. Some families hide behind their religious beliefs, or feel guilty about them, but others use their faith in healthy ways, to assist them in their personal growth and allow them to seek help for these complex situations. Simplistic answers or judgmental, legalistic dogmas are not helpful and make an already stressful situation even more disparaging. In this book, we'll explore personal faith in God as it relates to healing and restoration, as opposed to specific doctrines or sets of rules.

Ruth and Andy felt judged when they sought their answers in "religion." The simplistic answers they were given proved ineffectual in helping them deal with their family problems. They needed to realize that guidance is only as good as the counselor's knowledge and experience. One wouldn't go to a general practitioner for a specialized heart operation. Faith is not something we can obtain from someone else; it is something that we experience and seek for ourselves. Faith can involve the church or other people trained in theological matters, but it is ultimately our decision before God and involves our ongoing search and struggle.

■ *Separation and loss*

"Family" is the place where we all began. We needed a place to feel safe and secure, thus enabling us to develop and grow and launch a life of our own. Unfortunately, not many of us made the journey to adulthood without battle scars. And in the cases of blended families there are certain family casualties that precede the new family.

Two main issues underlie most of the problems in blended families: SEPARATION and LOSS. If you, as parents, can get to the root of those issues and help your children do the same, you can work out almost any of the day-to-day conflicts you face in your family. This by no means implies that things will be perfect, or that all your problems will be solved. You will, however, be better able to work things through, giving you and your children some powerful tools for dealing with your future lives.

Each person in a blended family must come to terms with his or her own sense of a separation from and loss of the first family. They have been separated from that family through divorce or death, and this is one of the most devastating losses anyone can experience. We all want to belong and to have permanent attachments in our lives. No one wants to lose his or her family. The family is our base of operations; it gives us our sense of who we are and provides the springboard from which we launch out to accomplish our goals in adult life. To lose this base of operations is tantamount to ripping the foundation out from under a house and attempting to leave the house standing.

The image we have of ourselves is largely formed from our family's treatment of us. The messages we received growing up about ourselves, our family's interactions, and life in general were ingrained in our minds, and they affect our way of relating to our present family and life.

A blended family comes in as a second team, in a sense, after much of the destruction has already taken place. There is no way an attempt can be made to make the house stand without redoing the foundation. The foundation is restored by processing the grief and unresolved issues from the previous family. This is not a popular thought, and it can be an overwhelming one, especially if the first family breakup was prolonged and messy. *The more losses and upheavals, the harder it will be to help the new family blend together.* It is never impossible, but one must be realistic and deal as honestly as possible with what has happened.

Many people going into a blended family want to forget and repress everything that happened before. To ignore the issues in your family is to bury a bomb in the basement and call it the foundation. There *will* be an explosion at some point.

Usually the children are a good barometer for what is happening in the family. Their behavior will clue you in on which problems need work. We adults have learned how to look good on the outside, but children are more honest in their actions. Often, difficult behavior signifies a need for help.

Signs of Separation and Loss

One of the most common results of separation is a feeling of sadness that brings about the grieving process. What are some of the other symptoms that you can notice in either yourself, your spouse, or your children? Any or all of the following may occur: sleeplessness, unexplained crying, depression, anger, outbursts, lethargy, lying, stealing, suicidal feelings and actions, hopelessness, eating problems, withdrawal, mood swings, unexplained or exaggerated fatigue. This is not an exhaustive list, and some of these symptoms may be rooted in other problems, but these are things to watch for.

When families start over, there are usually several members who are not finished working through their grief from the previous family. They are looking to the new family to resolve the grief for them. One person can never take another's place in our hearts and minds. It is crucial to go back and finish the grieving work in order to form a new attachment to the new family. The individual will then be free to accept the new family members for who they are, and the new family can be successful in the blending process.

This is not an instant process. Grieving takes time, and everyone grieves in a slightly different way. Realizing that the whole family is grieving will help you be more tolerant of each other and less apprehensive about what other members are going through.

Is there life after grieving? Or maybe we should ask, "Is there life during the grieving process?" Yes, blending a new family can take place at the same time as the grieving process—*if* the grieving is acknowledged.

The process of starting a new family is not unlike our first few months of life, when we grow secure in the love of our parents. A process occurs (or should occur) in which love, nurturance, emotional support, and, ultimately, the foundation for our personality is developed. We need to feel safe, cared for, and unconditionally loved, and we need to know that we will be accepted for who we are within our families. Of course, not everyone receives the proper love and care; some people are neglected and/or abused. Members of the new blended family who were not properly nurtured in their previous family need the opportunity to express their sadness—to grieve over those losses.

Which issues discussed in this chapter have surfaced in your family?

How did you identify them?

In what ways can you deal with them?

It is amazing what we can find under the surface if we look a bit more closely and ask some questions. Often we are not even aware of the issues that are affecting us and our families. It takes thought, prayer, and soul-searching to discover them. Half the battle is won when we acknowledge the existence of these issues and feelings and try to understand what they mean. Only then can we take action to work through and heal the wounds within our families.

3
My Bags Are Packed
Emotional Baggage and the New Family

Myra and Bill had dated for over a year before they decided to get married. They realized that their backgrounds would make it a challenge to bring their two families together. They received some premarital counseling, but they did not receive any *family* therapy before the marriage took place. Myra had been married before and had two boys, ages eight and five. Her husband, a decorated policeman, had been killed in the line of duty five and a half years earlier, and her younger boy had never known him. He had been verbally abusive to Myra and her older son and had threatened them with violent behavior.

Bill had been married for twelve years and had three girls, ages seventeen, fifteen, and twelve. When he met Myra, he had been divorced for five years and had been a recovering alcoholic for three years. His girls visited him every weekend, and they were very close to him. Although Bill had abandoned the family because of his drinking, when he entered a treatment program he tried to bring the family back together. But his wife had also begun to drink, and she did not want the relationship to continue. ■

25

> What questions do you think Bill and Myra would have about entering a marriage relationship and bringing their families together?
>
> What questions does their story bring up for you?

Bill and Myra's blended family is like a large case of explosives ready to be set off. Finding one another as lifelong companions and bringing their children together into a stable home may seem like a happy event, but the process is not easy. Each person coming into the new home brings along heavy baggage from life in the previous home.

Consider *your* blended family for a moment. Exactly who is involved in this new home? You and your spouse, your children and your spouse's children, along with the children who visit on the weekends, holidays, or other allotted times. Ex-spouses count as well, because they share your children with you. Even if they have abandoned the family or died, they are still members in the sense of being alive in the minds of those who remain. The *extended* family is also part of this happy group! Grandparents certainly do not want to be left out, and there may be as many as four sets. Now that you have determined who is in your family, think about what every person is carrying in his or her suitcase. In other words, what is each one feeling?

What Is Emotional Baggage?

Emotional baggage is any unresolved feelings you have about past events. Sometimes you or your children are aware of unresolved feelings, but often you aren't. None of us can escape these kinds of feelings because all of us have experienced painful events.

The emotional baggage you bring into your current family includes all the painful situations you encountered in your previous family that are the most difficult to talk about. Even if you have worked through some of the feelings and have accepted and come to terms with the events, the memories are still there. Possibly the new family triggers something you thought you had already worked through and set aside.

Another source of unresolved feelings comes from your _family of origin_, meaning the family you were born into. None of us grew up in a perfect family so we all carry some emotional pain into our adulthood. Often marriages fail because of the emotional baggage brought into the relationship by the husband and wife from their respective families of origin. Acknowledging these feelings helps you relate more directly to your current family.

Journeying back to old memories can be frightening, especially if you have spent a lifetime burying and denying all the pain you have experienced. Working through these feelings clears the way for the new blended family. You can't build a relationship with new family members if you still have unresolved feelings for previous family members and parents. But you can go through the healing process as you continue to build new relationships.

■ *Loss and trauma*

Two items that are sure to be found in every person's emotional "suitcase" are loss and trauma. In a blended family, separations cause many unresolved feelings. The more separations you or your children have experienced, the more difficult relationships are for you, because you may not believe that you can depend on their permanence. These separations cause sadness and a great sense of loss. Putting a new family together often triggers all the feelings of anger, disappointment, hopelessness, sadness, and loss that you felt when the previous family fell apart. Grief is at the core of this sense of loss. It is such a major aspect of emotional baggage that all of chapter 5 will explore the grieving process.

Trauma refers to any of the hurts you have experienced in your previous families. Traumas often go unrecognized and unresolved. If you or your children are victims of trauma, you may have buried hurts so deeply that you don't know on a conscious level that they exist. Or you may "act them out" in the new family because you are powerless to contain them.

Struggling with personal loss and trauma is normal. You enter the new family hoping to find healing and restoration, but you carry your hurts with you; they do not leave on their own.

■ *Identifying "baggage"*

So here it is, the moment each member of the family has either anticipated or dreaded. We are in our new home, our suitcases in our hands. It is time to unpack. We must take out what we have carried in with us, identify each item, and find a place for those feelings.

"Unpacking" means that we must identify all of those unresolved feelings. And for us to identify those feelings we must first ask ourselves what has happened to us to cause such feelings. We can't deal with the past until we thoughtfully explore our family history.

Most of us are not able to look at our history objectively enough to see some events for what they are. If your mother dies when you are nine and your younger siblings are six and three, it doesn't occur to you right away that you have become "mother" now. You may not realize for years that, in a sense, you were "deserted" by the person you depended on most. Growing up you may have only noticed that you had to work more around the house, and you often felt extreme loneliness. Once you can look back at your mother's death and see that it was a form of abandonment (not of her choosing, in this case), you can say to yourself, "I was left with huge responsibilities that a child should not have to carry." You can look at your feelings and find understandable reasons for them. You may even see that the role you play as an adult in your family is similar in that you are the caretaker for your family and friends. This is a first step in resolving those feelings. The emotions that hurtle through you stop being so mysterious and hard to deal with.

When people come to see me for therapy, I cannot help until I know the events that have caused their pain. All the memories are not at our fingertips—this is why therapy is sometimes necessary. But as we give ourselves permission to remember, more of our past becomes available to us.

Until we face past events and memories we cannot begin to create new memories and traditions. We end up spending so much time and energy trying to keep the old items from popping out of the suitcase that we are not free to deal with anything else—we cannot develop new and positive relationships.

Often one family member has to lead the way in helping the rest of the family discover their unresolved feelings.

Many times this person is the mother, because, frankly, women are "allowed" to express emotion more openly in our society. Women tend to be more aware of the way they feel. Men have been expected to keep their feelings to themselves in spite of their pain. Thankfully, this is changing in our society, but not quickly enough. So, perhaps Mother begins the process of discovering unresolved feelings. She and Dad work on their feelings together. As they begin to learn this new way of expression, they can lead the children to a deeper level of understanding, too.

Sometimes the blended family is pushed toward the "unpacking" process because one of the children develops behavioral problems at school or becomes depressed. Sometimes the statement that "a little child shall lead them" proves to be quite accurate. Parents are often more willing to heal their children's pain than their own. Whatever the case, the time comes when the need to unpack your bags is urgent. It's best if the parents set an example in dealing with unresolved feelings as soon as possible in order to help the family settle into life together.

Just because you are in pain doesn't mean you can't have a new family or that your dreams and hopes won't come true. But part of the process involves taking care of old hurts— unpacking your bags—and facing what you find. You have probably already discovered that this doesn't all happen at once. But as you struggle through emotions and come to some resolution and healing, more and more space is cleared for the new family relationships.

Back to Bill and Myra

Although this chapter will involve all members of the blended family, it will focus on the husband and wife since they offer the support and leadership of the family. If we can figure out some of their problems, then we can apply them to the rest of the family. As we look again to Bill and Myra's story, see which issues you identify with.

Bill and Myra returned home from their honeymoon to have his three girls descend on them for the first weekend in the new house. The girls weren't accustomed to sharing Bill with anyone, let alone another woman. And they were disgruntled at the idea of Myra's two sons living with their father full-time. The girls were sullen, uncooperative, and especially rude to Myra. When the girls left on Monday, Myra's boys reacted strongly to what had happened. Five-year-old Mike cried and clung to Myra and did not want to go to kindergarten. Dan, age eight, became sullen and withdrawn, staying in his room the entire time he was home from school.

Myra was angry with Bill for scheduling the girls' first visit so close to their homecoming. Bill was angry with Myra for not understanding that his girls needed a stable home environment. They went into their room to try and figure out what was happening. Myra cried and Bill paced. He was finally able to go over and sit on the bed next to her. They held each other in silence for a time and then voiced their disappointment at not having more time for each other. They decided to have a family meeting with the boys to help them understand what they were feeling. They also agreed to meet each other for lunch that week, to make sure they had time for the two of them to be alone. Bill decided to go to an extra Alcoholics Anonymous meeting to gain more support. Myra agreed to consider attending a wives' support group, a suggestion made by their premarital counselor.

Myra and Bill sat down with the two boys, saying they wanted to talk as a family, to help everyone work through their feelings. Upon hearing this, Dan got up from the table and started to leave the room. When Bill asked him to stay, Dan whirled around, knocked over a chair, and said, "You can't tell me what to do!" Bill responded by saying he would like to hear Dan's opinions and feelings. Dan stayed, but stood sullenly in a far corner of the room. Myra asked Dan if the weekend had reminded him of anything that had gone on with his father. At this point, Mike began to cry and crawled up into Myra's lap. Dan said yes, it had.

Bill asked Dan what had happened to upset him. Dan looked to Myra for help, and she indicated to him that it was all right to go ahead with the truth. He said that when Bill had yelled at his daughters for fighting, it had made him afraid that Bill would become violent, as his own father had. Bill assured Dan that he did not believe in physical violence. He encouraged Dan to tell him if he was ever afraid of what was happening. Myra said she wanted him to come to her if he felt he could not go to Bill, but she wanted him to feel safe enough to go to Bill with his honest feelings. Bill further explained that his girls were having a difficult time adjusting because there had been so many changes for them. He pointed out that the girls felt separated from their friends and school when they visited him and that they didn't have a stable home life because of their mother's alcoholism. He emphasized that this did not excuse the girls' rude behavior and that he would take the girls out that week and explain this to them.

Bill and Myra asked the boys if there could be a family meeting with the girls when they next visited so that every member's opinion could be heard and respected. The boys piped up and said that their contribution would be to put a sign on their bedroom door that read: No Girls Allowed! Everyone laughed, relieved—they had worked through a problem together. ■

How did Bill and Myra handle their own anger?

How did this help them deal with the anger of their children?

By interpreting the boys' behavior, Bill and Myra got to the root of the problem, and important issues were discussed. Each person's fears were dealt with, and they began their journey as a family unit. The boys saw that Bill was interested in getting to know them and was not just pulling rank and taking control. Bill and Myra admitted their feelings of frustration to each other, reached out to each other, and made plans to nurture their relationship as a couple. They all made plans, as a family, to set up some guidelines and boundaries so each member would know what to expect.

From this example it's easy to see that fear was part of the baggage brought into the new home. There was also a lot of anger. Many of our emotions fall into these two general categories. We fear many things, from a violent stepfather to our own loss of importance. When family members feel that they are being taken advantage of or that no one is listening to them, anger is the natural result.

The couple can feel anger when they have not had sufficient time together, whether in the form of a honeymoon or just within the family structure. They are not accustomed to dealing with some of the new children they are now parents to. We saw how Myra and Bill attempted to deal with their angry feelings in a constructive, healing way.

Four "Big Ones": Guilt, Jealousy, Privacy, and Sexuality

Four big items show up repeatedly in the blended family's luggage. We need to understand how they affect each person.

■ Guilt

Several factors usually trigger guilty feelings for the married couple. Guilt multiplies in the lives of those who have already been through one marriage. First of all, you as the new couple may feel guilty for being so happy with each other, particularly if your children and other family members are not as happy with the marriage as you are. You feel guilty for putting your happiness above that of other people close to you.

You may also feel guilty about your contribution to the breakup of your first marriage. The more unresolved issues from the previous family you have, the more guilt you feel now.

When your children have problems in the new family as a result of what has gone on before, you as parents will naturally carry guilt for those wounds.

Both Myra and Bill brought their share of guilt from their previous marriages. Myra had guilty feelings about her husband, who had died. Everyone in her family was lauding him as a hero and viewing his death as a tragedy. Myra felt guilty for telling the truth about his abusive behavior and the miserable life she had had with him. She kept these deep feelings locked in a secret place, and they magnified her guilt and made her feel worse about herself. It became difficult for her to tell what had really happened in their marriage because she did not have an outside support system or anyone who saw her deceased husband as anything less than a hero.

Myra's guilt made her keep her feelings a secret, creating shame and doubt about herself. When she was able to share with Bill, he reassured her that her feelings were normal. He affirmed her right to feel upset and angry about the abuse she had suffered. She could then talk to other women who had similar experiences and gain support and strength from them.

Bill felt guilty about his drinking and abandonment of his first family. He also felt badly about his ex-wife's drinking, believing that if he had not left the family, she wouldn't drink. These guilty feelings caused Bill to play "rescuer" to the girls. Every time they called, he went running over to solve their problems. He had never really separated from his previous family and was thus playing the "enabler" to his ex-wife's drinking.

Bill's guilty feelings tied him to his previous marriage, causing him to take on a role that was not healthy for him or the girls. It was important for him to support his girls and for them to know that they could come to him with their problems, but he needed to insist that his ex-wife get treatment and accept some responsibility for her daughters.

Bill was feeling guilty about his ex-wife's drinking, although he knew that it was not his responsibility. Bill needed to forgive himself for his past behavior and allow himself to grieve over the result of his actions rather than trying to punish himself further.

These different issues play off of one another, and we can feel more than one emotion at a time. Notice how quickly guilt, fear, or hurt can turn into anger or feed anger that is already there.

▣ *Jealousy*

Bill's girls were especially jealous of Myra because she was another woman who was taking their father away from them. They were also jealous of the boys, who got to live with their father full-time and receive the attention they did not have growing up. The boys, on the other hand, felt jealous of the girls because their biological father hadn't taken proper care of them. They wanted a chance to have Bill all to themselves. Myra was jealous of the girls, feeling that Bill was always leaving her and the boys to go help them. She was also jealous of Bill's ex-wife, whose drinking and irresponsible behavior took a toll on Bill and his current family. At those times, Myra felt almost as though Bill were still married to his ex-wife.

Bill was pulled in so many directions that he hardly had time to feel jealous. When he did, it was of Myra's relationship with the boys. She was more patient and loving with them than she was with him. She seemed to have a special bond with them that he could never share, and he felt hurt and left out.

What is the key to surviving jealous feelings? First of all, it helps to realize that these feelings arise out of wanting to belong to a family. In a blended family you do have to share children with the person or marriage that has gone before. It is normal to not want to share your new family with anyone else and want it to be special.

When certain family members have been together longer than others, talking about other people's family experiences can help to dissolve jealousy. The more people talk about their feelings, the more situations get worked out. There may be more conflict and hurt initially, but those feelings have to be aired. (And I'm not talking about cruel comments or name calling, but about genuine, personal feelings.)

For example, Myra could let the girls know that she understood how they felt about wanting their dad all to themselves.

By admitting that she also had jealous feelings she could work *with* them instead of being in constant competition with them. If Myra also talked to Bill about how she felt when he ran over to his ex-wife's house, maybe he would see his behavior as enabling her addiction and do something to change it. Bill could lessen some of his jealousy if he discussed with Myra how he felt about her closeness to the boys. Maybe then she could reassure him of her love and share his grief.

Talking is essential to working through family conflicts; it is the only way for you to know one another's feelings and motivations. Sometimes you must risk bringing up deeper, vulnerable feelings even if you fear misunderstanding or rejection. You can express how you feel and ask your spouse and children to do the same. Sometimes making a pact with the other person—before the discussion starts—is helpful. Agreeing to just listen and show acceptance of what each person is saying can assure them of the support needed to express these feelings.

Since members of a blended family have not lived together before, they are unaware of pre-existing relationships and don't know what emotions are going to be triggered by the formation of new alliances. Bill had not lived at Myra's house, so he did not know what it would be like to share her affections with her boys. Conversely, Myra had not lived with Bill, so she hadn't been as big a threat to his girls as when they had to visit in her new home. Alliances change when the marriage takes place, and family members are never fully prepared for how this will feel.

■ *Privacy*

Have you ever felt the walls of your house closing in on you? Have you ever felt like you wanted to run and hide, but there was no place to go? If so, you need your privacy!

Blended families do not always have this luxury. But privacy is not a luxury, especially in building a new family. It is a necessity!

Many times when members of a blended family come together, they are moving into a house with more than the original number of people. Children who previously had their own rooms now have to share full-time (or perhaps part-time on the weekends with visiting children) with other children they have never lived with before. The family room has now been turned into a bedroom. There are more people sharing the bathroom.

Privacy includes more than just living space.

When a family moves in together, boundaries must be drawn. There are the physical boundaries, involving the assignment of bedrooms and the naming of communal and private areas. Privacy has different meanings to different people, and some people need more privacy than others. The important thing is to decide together what the boundaries will be for the family.

The couple has their own room, but they have not had a chance to set up their boundaries with the rest of the family. The children are not used to living with a new couple and are testing their limits. Couples must first determine what their own boundaries and privacy needs are so that they can communicate that to the children. Couples must let the children know that they need some time together apart from other members of the family. Most couples find it difficult to express this need. They feel guilty and inattentive to the family if they spend time and money on themselves. Actually, the opposite is true. By showing the children what a healthy relationship is, you provide them with good role models. After recharging your own batteries, you will be better able to deal with the stresses of the family.

After six months of marriage, Myra and Bill decided to go away for the weekend. They decided that the girls could take care of the boys since they were all getting along. They needed to spend some time developing their relationship and explained this to the children. Myra's mother agreed to stay with the children and make supper. But she was under strict instructions *not* to contact the couple unless it was a matter of life and death. When Myra and Bill got home, the girls were upset that they had not been able to contact Bill over the weekend. The following week they called and invented reasons for him to come over. Bill made arrangements to take them out alone the following Saturday but told them that he could not come over every time they called. He explained that he loved them and wanted to be there for them but, if they wanted to be part of the family and not just visitors, they had to be considerate of the needs of all the family members. He also explained that if they wanted him to be less tired and worried, then he needed some time to himself to relax. They agreed, with some reservations.

Originally, Bill had difficulty agreeing to go away and leave his daughters. He realized that his guilt had origins that went farther back than his drinking days. He started to remember what it was like for him growing up and why he was so hesitant to give himself some time and space. Bill's father was an alcoholic who had not been available to him. His mother overcompensated for this by being too protective of Bill, demanding that all his time be accounted for and all her needs met. As a result, Bill never was allowed to have a life of his own. He realized that the main reason he went away with Myra for the weekend was not to relax but to make Myra happy. Not a bad reason, but it failed to meet his needs. ■

This is a prime example of how important it is to probe those unresolved feelings from childhood. If Bill had not allowed himself some privacy, these feelings might not have surfaced.

When you give yourselves privacy as a couple and as individuals, you can work out emotions that may have been hidden for years. Take time for meditation, prayer, and relaxation to help you deal with the problems that your new family life presents. Don't let emotional baggage clutter the blending process.

■ *Sexuality*

Sexuality is a difficult issue to address in any family, but it is even more difficult to deal with in a blended family. We learn about sexuality and how to express it from our family of origin. Often, sexuality is not talked about openly in families, and we try to deny that children have any curiosity about a subject that makes us so uneasy.

The couple in a blended family often forfeits a honeymoon due to the various factors of children, time, and money, sacrificing a valuable opportunity to be alone and discover each other. Even with that time alone, coming home to a house with little eyes watching every move does put a damper on new love!

Another potential problem in blended families is the issue of the children's ages and genders. If the children of your two families are the same age or close to it, prepubescent, adolescent, and of the opposite sex, you may have a powder keg on your hands. Since these children did not grow up together, the incest taboo is not as strong as in the original family. Sex education and boundaries must be stressed. Uncomfortable feelings may also arise if a stepparent is younger and therefore closer to the age of the teenage children.

All of these factors put a strain on you as a couple because it is difficult to know how to express your affection for your new mate in front of the children. One couple put a lock on the inside of the bedroom door and installed a stereo system so that they could have privacy and block out the family's noise.

You also have to be more watchful of the children and educate them so they will be safe from inappropriate behavior. The temptation, of course, is to sweep everything under the carpet and pretend that uncomfortable issues are nonexistent. But ignoring problems won't help to solve them.

FAMILY STORY

One evening when Bill's girls were visiting for the weekend, his fifteen-year-old daughter came prancing out into the living room in a skimpy nightgown, much to the shock of Bill and the boys. Bill ordered her to go to her room and put some clothes on. She did, accompanied by much giggling from all the children.

Bill and Myra decided to talk to her. Initially, Bill did most of the talking. He asked her if she was still hoping that he and her mother would get back together, and she affirmed this. He said he knew it was difficult for her to see him and Myra together. He stated that he did not want her to feel she had to act in this manner to get attention from boys, whether it was her brothers or boyfriends. He said he hoped she would wait until she was with someone in a permanent marriage before she fully expressed herself. He also suggested that maybe she and

41

Myra could read some sex-education books together. Hearing this, she made a face, but Myra spoke up and said that she would like to go out shopping for a book, have lunch, and talk about some of these things.

Bill and Myra then had similar but separate conversations with the boys and the other two girls. Finally they retreated to their own room, not knowing whether to laugh or cry. ■

Many times in families it is difficult to know what is normal behavior and what is inappropriate behavior. This example falls between the lines, depending on what is going on in the family. It is normal for children of all ages to explore sexual boundaries in an attempt to understand what is acceptable behavior.

Try to identify times in your family when guilt, jealousy, privacy, or sexuality issues surfaced.

What happened, and how did you respond?

Is there a different way you could have handled it?

How can you prepare for future incidents?

Education and dialogue are the two keys to dealing with a difficult subject.

- You and your mate first must identify what your sexual issues are and what you have to work on. Many times if couples are not satisfied with their own sexuality it is more difficult to address these matters.

- You must determine your own values and beliefs about sexuality before you can teach your children.

- Discuss sexual matters with your children, educating them at appropriate levels for their ages. Never assume that they are too young to be taught. A little information at a time from the very beginning is best.

Bill and Myra operated as a team and stated their values, but they did not condemn, judge, or make sex a taboo or dirty subject. They also tied the sexual issues to the larger picture of Bill's daughter wishing to see her parents back together. In this way they opened the door for her to grieve for the loss of her parents' relationship instead of having to act it out sexually. It gave her and Myra a chance to bond, providing a good beginning in the family-blending process.

You need courage to deal with these complex sexual matters, but they are a vital part of the emotional baggage that must be worked through in order for everyone to feel comfortable in the new home environment.

Incorporating New Information

As a new family, it is impossible to know everything about the people you are living with. Even if no information has been intentionally withheld, it's still difficult to be in touch with all of your memories or to share them all with your mate before marriage. In a first marriage, some of these feelings come to the surface during everyday events and are then dealt with. How many of us have said to our mate, "I never knew you felt that way"?

In a blended family, feelings may surface in similar ways, but they can trigger a bigger reaction because there are more people involved and the couple has not had a chance to process some of these issues on their own. The family has not bonded together yet so everyone is more guarded than in a household where everyone has lived together from the start.

FAMILY STORY

Bill began to develop rules for the girls during their visits. These included curfews, chores, and respectful behavior towards all members of the family. One night the seventeen-year-old daughter ran off and stayed away the entire night. Bill and Myra were frantic and called the police, as well as Bill's ex-wife. She told them that the girl had run away once before, after Bill had left the family.

When they finally found his daughter the next day, Bill talked with her about the reason for running away and asked her if she had ever run away before. She blurted out that she had once before when her mother got drunk and brought a man home. The man had made some sexual remarks to her that had frightened her, and so she ran away because she did not feel safe. Bill was enraged at his ex-wife for the danger she had put his daughters in, and Myra was also upset. They told the daughter they were glad she had confided in them and that they wanted her to tell them if she felt at any time that she or the other girls were in danger. They told her that they would talk to the other girls to see how they felt about what had happened with the man; they would also talk with her mother. They stressed that she needed to pick a safer way to express her feelings and not put herself in danger by running away.

After Bill's daughter got settled back at the house, Myra was still upset. The daughter's leaving had triggered a memory for her that she had not shared with Bill. She told him there was a time, several years before her husband was killed, when she had left him because he had been so verbally abusive and threatening that she couldn't take it anymore. She had gone and stayed with her mother, and her mother had told her that she had to go back with her husband and make it work. Myra, with no job or money, finally went back to him, only to have the situation become worse.

Bill was upset because he was on overload after having just dealt with his daughter and because he felt that Myra had not trusted him with the new information. He was not upset that she had left her husband but that she had not shared it with him while they were dating. Myra explained that she had been afraid he would think less of her and possibly not marry her if he had known. Bill felt badly for his daughter and Myra, as well as helplessly overwhelmed because he could not erase what had happened to them. Myra explained to him that they did not want him to solve everything, but simply be there to listen and give comfort. She added that when they were thinking more clearly in the morning they could make some decisions about what to say to his ex-wife.

Bill did, in fact, talk to his ex-wife the next day and insist that she get treatment for her drinking. He also decided to take the girls to Ala-teen, a group support for children whose parents drink. ■

What happens in a family when traumatic new information comes out? It upsets the family system and confronts people with the way they have been handling things in the past. This is sometimes necessary if change is to take place and bring the family closer. Hidden problems stand in the way of getting to know what kind of a life each person in the family has experienced. New information brings up a lot of emotion, but this is necessary to make way for new relationships and healing.

Bill realized that he could no longer play the rescuer role and had to make a healthy choice with his ex-wife that allowed their daughters to deal with her drinking. It also gave him the freedom to be more available to Myra. Instead of feeling guilty, he could help her deal with her past and be more available for her.

Couples go through many situations when entering into a blended family.

What problems are specific to your experience and your family?

Take some time to look back on incidents that you remember and see what emotional baggage exists within your family. Maybe it's time to unpack those bags and start to deal with their contents.

What Triggers Your Problems?

No one book or person can give you a magic formula on how to unpack your emotional baggage. Beware of people with formula answers! The examples in this chapter point out that each person has unresolved feelings that still need to be processed.

Remember that what happens in your blended family triggers complicated issues for all members, depending on what they have been through in their pasts. Many times there are ongoing memories of the previous marriages—visitation rights or damage to the children—that add to an already explosive family situation. Are there any current problems in your family that may contribute to your emotional baggage?

The following principles may be effective in helping your blended family unpack their bags and settle in together.

1. Identify the problem

2. Identify the feelings associated with the problem

3. Identify what feelings are triggered from previous families

4. Identify feelings from the family of origin

5. Work on feelings through support, comfort, and prayer

There often comes a point in therapy when a person has explored difficult issues and has identified many of the feelings involved, yet is still unable to begin working through an active recovery program. At this point, I ask the question that I am asking you now: What is stopping you?

I encourage people to develop a program that will help them identify their feelings, find support, and develop a spiritual connection that goes deeper than themselves. Here are some steps that I've found to be helpful for this process.

■ *Discover what helps you.*

Whatever you recognize as therapeutic to you—talking to a friend, writing, long walks, hot baths, music, reading, exercise—do it. Research on stress has shown that even two fifteen-minute relaxation periods a day are helpful in reducing stress, lowering blood pressure, and giving a better sense of well-being. Start there and see how much better you feel.

■ *Try to identify your specific feelings.*

What are you feeling in your blended family now, and what does this trigger from the family, or families, you were involved with before this one? What feelings can you trace back to the family you grew up in? How do you get in touch with these feelings? How can you know from which family they are derived?

The process of journal writing can be most helpful in sorting out feelings that pour in from different sources. To journal is simply to write down your feelings in some form. If something is upsetting you and you can't figure out what it is, you may find that writing about the incident helps you identify your feelings. It provides an outlet for the emotions and gives you many clues as you look back over what you have written. Some people are afraid of what feelings may come out, but this is a contained, safe way of discovering and examining your emotions. The experience can be very liberating, yet you have significant control over how far it goes.

◼ *Get support.*

Start to let other people into your life at a deeper level. You cannot carry those heavy bags around with you for the rest of your life, so let others help you. What kind of support do you need? It is essential to make time with your spouse for learning how to be supportive of one another's feelings. Friends are also important. Sometimes friends who are going through or have been through some of the same struggles can provide the most help and support. You are not looking for someone to tell you what to do, but to be sensitive and understanding. A support group of people who are going through similar problems can also help. Classes on parenting, self-esteem, and problem solving, to name but a few, can be good, especially for people who are just beginning to learn what their feelings are.

◼ *Make use of prayer and meditation.*

More will be said about this in chapter 9, but it is important that you provide time for your own spiritual renewal. Refreshing your own relationship with God is a crucial way to give you the insight and strength you need. You need to recognize that you can't always solve your own problems. God is a friend and a source of strength for you. Reach out and begin your spiritual journey. Even if you have always attended church, prayed every day, and thought you knew all the appropriate theology, there are always new spiritual depths to explore, especially at a time when you are struggling to build a new family.

◼ *Plan spouse time and family time.*

Spend some time alone with your spouse every week, discussing these issues. Many times in the morning before we get up and start the day, my husband and I will discuss our dreams for the future or other related emotional issues. You need time to connect with your spouse in this way; it bonds the two of you together. Also take time each week for the family to be together to talk, to process feelings, and to see who is hurting or feeling worried. Schedules are jammed, I know, but these family times must be given priority over outside activities if your household is to bond together.

In the process of unpacking those bags, the family can become closer. We can learn more about ourselves and understand each person better. And this makes way for the growth of family bonding and intimacy, the subject of the next chapter.

4
Who Can I Feel Close To?
Achieving Family Intimacy

FAMILY STORY ONE

Jane and Henry had been married several years when their first baby, Mark, was born. Mark was a happy baby, and both Henry and Jane loved to rock him and sing to him. Henry would hold him high in the air and bounce him on his lap until Mark laughed. When Mark was about a year old, Jane and Henry decided they would like another child.

When Jane became pregnant again, the road was not as easy as it had been with Mark. Jane's morning sickness seemed worse, she was more uncomfortable, and she gained weight faster than with her first baby. Her discomfort kept her from being as available to Mark as she had been in the past. Shortly before Mark's second birthday, baby Ann was born prematurely. Colicky and underweight, she did not have Mark's winsome ways. Henry was very concerned about both Jane and Ann when they came home from the hospital. Jane seemed so much more tired than she had been with Mark. Ann was small and sickly and cried much of the time. In all the confusion, Henry and Jane had not had time to prepare Mark for the birth of his sister. He had stayed with Henry's mother for the week Jane had been in the hospital, and she was considerably stricter than Henry and Jane.

Upset by all of the changes that were occurring in his household, Mark cried often and tried to cling to Jane when she was holding the baby. At times he would throw himself on the floor

51

and have a tantrum. Henry and Jane felt they were under siege and wondered what had happened to their ideal, happy family. ■

Has your family had experiences that are similar to Henry and Jane's?

How is your situation the same or different from theirs?

Although the above story is not about a blended family, it clearly illustrates issues connected with bonding and family closeness. Each family has its own ideas about intimacy and how it should be accomplished. When the closeness in the first family has already broken, people erect many defenses against becoming close to members of the blended family.

What Is Bonding?

We hear a lot about "bonding": everything from the mother-infant relationship to a group of men getting together to experience their maleness through story-telling and drum playing. *Bonding* simply means "attaching," and it usually refers to a parent or other significant person.

Bonding begins for each of us with our relationship to our mother at birth. The newborn infant is in a helpless state, dependent on another person for all his needs. Some of these needs are physical: to be fed, changed, kept warm, and transported from one place to another. But the emotional needs of the infant are equally important. These have to do with the infant's deep need for love and nurture. Studies show that babies who have had all of their physical needs met but who have not had any human contact in the way of singing, holding, or rocking, fail to do well and can even die in some cases.

At first, the infant does not distinguish between herself and the mother as being two separate people. Gradually she starts to distinguish her own separateness, and self-awareness is born. This close relationship between mother and child helps the infant to feel safe and tell the difference between pleasure and pain. The mother's activities of holding, singing, talking to, and making eye contact with the child, especially during feeding, help the child bond with the mother. Some people call this process "attachment." Bonding helps the child begin to experience her inner self as part of the mother and then as something unique to herself. This initial bonding is crucial and must be repeated symbolically by the new blended family as it is being born.

Jane's nurturing of baby Mark was a primary example of bonding. Henry's affection for his infant son was a good example of a father attaching to his new son.

The bonding process is the foundation for our personality and adult life. How well we did or did not bond in those first personal relationships has a great effect on how well we bond or don't bond with our new blended family. The lack of bonding in the beginning may contribute to later separations making trust for new relationships a bigger challenge.

You can see how happy Mark was when things were going well and his mother was available to him. You can also see how upset he was when the bonding process was interrupted and changed through the birth of his sister. Life presents many circumstances along the way to interrupt or inhibit the bonding process.

What Are Some of the Steps in the Bonding Process?

■ *A baby learns to distinguish between pleasure and pain as she bonds with her mother.*

The mother is the defender against pain and the manager of painful experiences. Because the mother handled pain for the helpless infant, the older child learns to survive and gains some control over her environment and even her own behavior as she grows older.

Have you ever had the experience of warming a bottle for a screaming baby who was right there beside you and could see what you're doing but was too young to understand that food was on the way? The mother, at this point, is managing the pain for the infant. The infant has no control over her crying and has no concept of what is being done or how to manage the pain of hunger.

■ *The child learns about relationships and develops into a social being.*

The bond with the mother helps the baby learn to depend on relationships with people and to see them in a healthy, positive light.

■ *The child is able to establish a relationship with himself, and then with the outside world.*

The child can use the relationship with his mother to help him feel secure so that he can venture outside the relationship into the world and then have a safe place to come running back to when he becomes frightened or insecure. Have you ever seen a toddler run away from his mother with great delight only to get a distance away from her and then panic? He wanted to practice feeling independent, yet still needed the safety of his mom. If the mother does not allow this exploration or does not greet the child's return with support and delight, the child then receives conflicting messages about the mother's support or the validity of venturing out and becoming an independent person.

What Does This Have to Do with a Blended Family?

The way you grow and develop from birth onward has everything to do with how you will respond to marriage and family life. Your beginnings in this life are only as good as the abilities, circumstances, and experiences of the family you were born into. If you experienced separations instead of bonding, you will play that out in your adult relationships in one way or another.

At this point, you may be thinking that everything that goes wrong in the family is your parents' fault. That's not true! We give our children the best we have to give. What we cannot give them is what we were not given ourselves, and we need to realize this in order to forgive both ourselves and our parents.

■ *Integrating others*

According to Erik Erickson, a renowned child therapist, the child learns to trust or mistrust during the first year of life. The child also begins interpersonal relationships at that time. The child's greatest anxiety at this stage of development is the fear of abandonment. Erickson goes on to point out that the development of trust is followed by the beginning of some sense of independence and the capacity for restraint of inner drives and aggressions. This results in respect for out-side demands and authority.

Children need consistent role models and caretakers who will enable them to bond and develop trust. There is no trust without bonding. I see this in the children I work with in a children's home where there is a high turnover in staff. These children do not have one primary caretaker and have already been abused or abandoned by their natural parents. They have trouble trusting, building relationships, and respecting the rules of society.

Bonding and trust are well-known subjects, but how do they apply to the blended family? And why is it so difficult initially for the family to bond?

■ *Why is bonding so difficult?*

Separations cause a break in the bonding process, no matter the age of the child and parent. Blended families have already gone through a number of separations when they begin the bonding process with the new family. All members of the family have at least a degree of anxiety about bonding to each other, fearing disappointment or further abandonment. The bonding process takes longer and is fraught with more obstacles due to the number of previous separations.

FAMILY STORY TWO

John and Beth took John's ten-year-old son, Allan, for coun-seling because he was depressed, was not eating or sleeping, and was starting to have problems concentrating on his school work. They had been married the year before, and Beth had a three-year-old daughter named Sarah. At first the two children had gotten along rather well, but then Allan had begun to tease Sarah. Both parents disciplined Allan very strictly, and the teasing stopped. But the depression seemed to build from that point on.

John and his first wife, Allan's mother, had been divorced since Allan was five. When he was seven, his mother married a man with whom Allan did not get along, and they moved to another state. Allan missed his father and begged to go live with him. After the mother had another child by her current husband, she let John have custody of Allan. Three years later, Allan's father married Beth, who also had a younger child. ■

What bonds have been broken in Allan's life?

How many times has he attempted to attach to someone new?

Let's look at the history of bonding and separation for Allan.

1. Allan had his initial separation from his father and the break in the bond of his biological family when he was five.

2. He then re-bonded with his mother, and the two of them constituted a family of their own. He lost that exclusive bond when his mother married her second husband.

3. Allan then attempted—in a negative way—to bond with the man his mother married. This bond was broken in two ways when Allan's mother had another child and gave up custody of Allan to his father.

4. Allan then rebonded with his father when he went to live with him for three years. That bond was disrupted when John married Beth.

5. Allan tried to bond with this new family, again in a negative way, by teasing his new sister. When John and Beth dealt with him so harshly, they reminded him of the other broken bonds. No wonder Allan was depressed!

Must parents forfeit their chances for remarriage and a new start? No, that is not the point. The emphasis in the family should be on understanding the bonding process and helping each member work through his or her own grief over the previous separations.

You can see from the example how most blended families have had several separations before they come to the family. The first separation of the biological family breaks the strongest initial bonding outside of our own bonding with our parents. The family we grew up in and the family that we first marry into are the two initial and strongest bonds we experience. After death or divorce, another bonding process goes on in the single-parent family. Not only does the parent-child relationship shift due to the loss of the other parent, but sometimes there is additional bonding to the people who enter family life as supporters, such as close friends and relatives who help the parent and child go on after the break in the family. With the blended family comes yet another bonding experience. It isn't hard to see why blended families have such a difficult time in bonding together. They are all asking each other to believe there could be another family to trust.

A child's initial bonding with the mother forms the building blocks for trust in himself and the outside world. When the biological family breaks up, the bond that has been the basis for life is broken. Even if a child still lives with his mother or sees her regularly, the bond that taught him about being close to another person is broken. He must then go through a period of grieving for the loss of that bond and for the fact that no other bond will ever be able to take the place of the biological mother and family. He may then, in time, learn a new type of trust that is based on a sense of self and a personal faith. This is especially difficult for young children who do not yet have the reasoning power to figure out what is happening to them. Young children think concretely; either Mom is here or she's not. All the reasons in the world for the separation don't change the emotional reaction within the child.

What happens in the blended family when the bonding process falters? We have seen that blended families have trouble bonding because of previous separations and emotional baggage. Allan, in our family story, tried to bond with his stepfather and stepsister by "regressing"—returning to earlier forms of behavior as an attempt to solve a problem.

■ *What are some of the feelings triggered by the new bonding process that may cause problems?*

Anxiety. When there is a threat of loss we feel anxious. When we have had a number of losses we learn to become anxious at every disruption, and we are "on guard" for any possible threat. Allan demonstrated his anxiety by teasing his sister.

Grief. When the family has gone through a divorce and no longer exists as a family unit, each member experiences some sort of grieving period.

Anger. When there is an actual loss, or the threat of a loss, anger plays a predominant role in the emotions of each person in the family. In our story, we saw Allan's anger at his stepfather.

Each of these emotions is triggered again when the blended family comes together. Long-forgotten memories and painful experiences float to the surface. Children regress to behaviors they demonstrated at the time of the first family breakup. For example, one five-year-old girl in therapy regressed to the speech and voice of her three-year-old self when describing her parent's divorce.

Adults in a blended family often report that feelings resurface around issues concerning their ex-spouses. These emotional issues often are displaced onto the child of that marriage. The child ends up getting blamed if the parents are not aware of their own emotional baggage. Sometimes a child will behave in a way that reminds the parent of the ex-spouse. To blame the child only creates further distance and inhibits bonding.

A woman sought therapy because her teen-age son was being disrespectful to her new husband and was not caring for himself or his possessions at school or at home. His mother was very angry at him. When we explored the situation further, we uncovered her anger at her ex-husband—the boy's father—for his neglect of his family. She remarked that her son was becoming "just like his father." We discovered that she was anxious about getting closer to her new husband for fear he would disappoint her the same way her ex-husband had. Both mother and son had regressed into behaviors characteristic of previous family situations.

Negative bonding can play a part in the bonding process. If emotional baggage comes into the new family without being processed, a member of the family, particularly a child, may behave in an inappropriate way in an attempt to bond with the family. Allan displayed negative bonding by teasing his stepsister. He was still grieving over the loss of his father to a new wife, yet he wanted to belong to the family. He tried to bond by using negative behavior because affection and caring made him too vulnerable to loss. The problem with negative bonding is that often the hurting person is labeled as a troublemaker. Family members then displace their own feelings onto that person, and the real problems are ignored.

Now that we understand some of the reasons blended families have trouble bonding, how do we encourage bonding in the new family?

Becoming a Part of the Family

Even the person in your blended family who most resists becoming a member still wants to be part of a family. How then do you as the parents and the couple help the family bond together?

Just as a mother bonds with her newborn baby, there must be a bonding process that happens between each new member of the family. In many ways bonding is more difficult in the blended family than with a new baby, who is totally dependent on you. The members of your family may seem unwilling at first, but you must try to discover ways of bonding with them and modeling ways to bond with each other. A tough assignment!

■ *Start by trying to find out what is meaningful to everyone involved.*

What makes them feel as if they belong? Ask them to educate you as to what makes them feel a sense of home.

61

■ *Try to find out what broke the bond for them
in the previous family.*

Discover their hurts—but don't try to fix them. Just listen, be
understanding, and refrain from passing judgement, especially
on another parent. Tell them you are sorry they have had so
much upheaval and pain. Let them know that you understand
they did not ask to be in this family and maybe are not sure they
want to be even now.

■ *Try to reassure them of your caring.*

Be realistic; do not promise them your love if you do not
have those feelings yet. You can talk about caring and still be
working on your own issues. Say that you would like for both
of you to learn to care about each other, and ask for some
suggestions as to how they think that can happen. Don't press
if you don't get an answer right away.

■ *Try to provide the atmosphere or the actions that
family members identify as making them feel
that they belong.*

For example, if the child says he likes to be read to before
bed, then read to him. Reassure him that you are not trying to
take the other parent's place; you just want to make him feel
that he belongs. Again, keep asking, "What made you feel
like you belonged in your previous family?" Don't press if
the child rejects you, but keep trying, maybe with actions
instead of questions.

Interestingly enough, we get very excited when a newborn
baby gives the slightest response to us, but we don't expect
this baby to get up and take out the garbage. Yet, *in a blended
family, because many times the children are older, we expect
them to move right in and fall into a family pattern. This is a*

newborn family and needs to be seen as such. You have a right to expect certain things from each individual, but, emotionally, you cannot expect bonding before the family has had time to live together and become close.

◼ *Make yourself available.*

When a new mother is at her baby's beck and call, she is in a sense "used up" by the baby. In other words, she is aware that the child has basic needs that she must attend to, no matter what else is happening in the rest of her life. I have heard many parents in blended families talk about their feelings of being "used" by their children's constant demands. Although children should not be allowed to take advantage of you, they do have many needs at this time. For example, one stepmother knew her stepson was perfectly able to get to school on the bus, but she also knew that he was having trouble relating to her and to the people at his new school. She would often offer to drive him to school, but only when it seemed appropriate or she had no other commitments. During that time, they had a chance to talk, listen to his favorite radio station, or just be together. This began to build the relationship between the two of them in a way that might not have happened otherwise. Parents sometimes worry that they're spoiling their children, but by withholding their time and affection they often miss their children's needs.

What makes you feel like someone is available to you? What makes you want to call a particular friend when you need help? What is it about that person that makes you feel that she will be there for you—what specifically does she do? The answers to these questions may be different depending on the person, but they will give you a clue about what being available to your family means.

■ *Be genuine with yourself and other members of the family.*

You do not have to be the perfect parent in order to bond, and you are not required to play the rescuer or the helper role in your family.

How can you be genuine? Don't attempt to fake something that you don't feel. If you don't get along with someone in the new family, try to figure out your emotional baggage and own it as yours. Say that your goal is caring, yet don't promise caring that you don't feel. You can try to make the person feel he belongs while you work on gaining your "bonding" feelings.

Many times blended families think they have to act the way they think a perfect family "should." I encourage families to find what is comfortable for them and to act accordingly. One woman was having trouble with her two teenage stepchildren. She was intimidated by them, while they feigned indifference to her. I encouraged her to discuss with them how they would like to see their family develop. She stated that she would like them all to care about one another, but she felt like she did not know them. She wanted to know their ideas for ways to get closer to them without making them feel crowded. The kids responded with skepticism and reserve, and it took several meetings to get a dialogue going. Finally, they began to suggest things offhandedly about coming to a school concert or helping them with projects, just to see what her response would be. She had to listen carefully to pick up on the cues and avoid overenthusiasm while still showing her pleasure and willingness to help. This may sound contrived, but it shows that you can have respect for everyone's feelings while being true to your own.

■ *Allow autonomy.*

Parents of the blended family want so much for the family to come together and be a unit that they sometimes demand a false sense of togetherness. Children and adults need freedom that is appropriate for their ages. Many times children from single-parent families have more freedom and responsibility for their age because their only parent has had to spend much of their time at work, leaving the children on their own.

Families need to be aware of levels of freedom their children have been allowed. They need to set appropriate limits for the children, but they cannot expect those who have had certain freedoms to give them all up for the new family.

Ten-year-old Chad was used to coming home from school to an empty house and starting dinner for his mom, who was at work. He did his homework, or didn't do it, depending on his mood. His grades were average, but nothing special. He was not supposed to go out of the house once he got home, but he did anyway from time to time. When his mother married Ted, she cut down to working part-time so she could be home with Chad and Ted's eight-year-old son. Chad had a difficult time adjusting to some of the new rules. He was used to monitoring his own time, but with his mother's more frequent supervision he started to rebel. He refused to do what she asked, became sassy, and would sometimes disappear for several hours. He and his mom had to sit down and develop new guidelines for his behavior. His mom asked if he would like to make dinner one night, or help other nights, so he wouldn't feel left out of the process. He agreed, and grew more cooperative.

Not only did Chad enjoy his freedom, but it symbolized for him the time he and his mother had constituted a family. He had lost this exclusive relationship with her when she remarried. But what his mother did integrated the old freedom and made him feel that he wasn't losing everything, yet still gave him appropriate limits for his age.

You can't change all the guidelines at once or expect the children and other members of the family to give up everything they had in the previous family. If you act sensitively and make it clear that you do not want to take away everything, you will get more cooperation, and bonding will take place much faster.

Adults also need their freedom. I encourage parents to have their own undisturbed time, as well as couple time, every week. You must preserve your bond as a couple if you are to lead the family effectively. Take time to replenish yourself and discover the changes you need to make to bond with this new family.

5
What Does It Mean to Grieve?
Separation and Loss

Ann and Hal had been dating for a number of years, and each had children who were in high school or college. They decided to marry and found the children unopposed to their union. Hal had two children, twenty-five-year-old Sam and nineteen-year-old Denise. Ann also had two children, an eighteen-year-old daughter, Haley, who was going away to college, and a sixteen-year-old son named David, who would be living with the couple after they were married.

On the day of the wedding all the children attended the ceremony. Both girls were obstinate, sitting in opposite corners of the room, giving everyone the silent treatment. Hal was upset with the girls for treating Ann with such disrespect, but Ann tried to smooth the waters by saying they had some things to work through. Eventually the boys' helpfulness brought the girls around.

The honeymoon couple went away for several weeks, and the girls took care of Hal's house, where the couple and Ann's son would be living. Everyone seemed encouraged and looked forward to the future.

When Ann and Hal returned from their honeymoon, Ann's son, David, had already moved into Hal's house, and both girls also stayed there for another month until they went back to their respective colleges.

Hal's daughter, Denise, felt she was abandoning her family when she went back to school. Hal discovered that she had phoned her mother long-distance every day while her father was away.

On the other hand, Ann's daughter, Haley, was very combative and had trouble even getting along with David, to whom she had always been close. She stated openly that she could not wait to go back to college and be on her own for good.

Hal's son, Sam, who was living and working on his own, did not contact the couple after their honeymoon, and repeated messages on his answering machine went unheeded. Throughout the turmoil, Ann's son, David, remained helpful and consoling to all members of the family. ■

How can you tell that the members of Ann and Hal's family were grieving?

What has happened in your family that has led you to believe that some of the members are going through their own grieving process?

What Is Grieving?

We define *grieving* as a reaction to any sense of loss, be it real or anticipated. The resulting reactions to this state of anxiety are also part of the grieving process.

Many times when we talk about grieving we relate it to someone's death. In the blended family, the previous families have "passed away" in their pre-existent forms, taking with them part of each person.

Grief, however, can encompass many other types of losses. Ultimately, death is the origin of our grieving, but the losses take on many forms. There are also different stages to the grieving process.

When we experience loss at a deep level it can trigger the memory of former losses. As we discussed in the chapter on bonding, blended families have experienced the breaking of the bonds from previous families. Those are the losses that cause the grieving process.

Our grieving originates in losses that took place in the family we grew up in. When we were little, our mothers would sometimes have to leave us behind when they went shopping. To a very young child who does not understand that the mother is coming back, she has gone away forever. The child may then become inconsolable. We also saw in the last chapter how many times the bonds can be broken in the normal growing-up process. Young children experience loss each time they are separated from their mothers and fathers. For most children, the bond with the mother is the first and closest one.

What takes place in a child's mind and heart when there is separation from the mother?

Separation anxiety. The child becomes very anxious at the first inkling of the mother's departure. The feelings of anxiety crescendo at the actual separation.

Despair. A hopelessness that results in grief and mourning, stemming from the child's belief that the mother will never return.

Detachment and defense. The child then experiences the detachment between himself and the mother and begins to emotionally distance himself from the mother.

To cope with the pain of this break, the child develops what we call defenses. The child may become hostile, clinging, or seemingly devoid of emotions. Even when the mother returns after only a short separation, the child may not at first welcome her affection.

In the case of this blended family, the girls, Denise and Haley, with their silent attitudes at their parents' wedding ceremony, were grieving over the loss of their previous families. Their silence was a good example of detachment. If we looked further into their backgrounds, we would see how both were separated for periods of time from their mothers. Old losses are indeed triggered by new ones.

David's helpfulness and scurrying around to meet everyone's needs showed his immense anxiety over the loss of his previous family structure. Hal's older son was also showing his despair over a new family beginning without him. Since he had already moved out of the house, he felt excluded. He demonstrated this by not contacting the family in any way, thus walling himself off with his grief.

It is clear, then, that losses experienced in our lives trigger the grieving process, starting in our formative years with the separations from our mothers. At each developmental stage in our lives we experience the losses in different forms. Children sometimes state that they feel like a part of them dies each time they are asked to give up what they had in a previous family. There is great sadness, pain, anger, and shame in loss. These feelings markedly affect the way we see ourselves and the world around us.

These losses also affect the development of our personality and self-esteem. It explains why some people spend their entire lives trying to make restitution to themselves and others for the losses they have experienced. They desperately need to find a way of building a bridge back to the bond that has been broken.

Through the grieving process we experience and work through the pain of our losses. We cannot rectify the losses until we have allowed ourselves to grieve.

Stages of Grieving

John Bowlby, a noted English psychiatrist and analyst, talks about the grieving process in stages that may apply very well to the blended family and their feelings of loss. He states that he feels there are three stages to normal grieving: (1) "The urge to recover the lost object"; (2) "Disorganization"; and (3) "Reorganization as an adaptive process" (Bowlby, pp. 333-335). Let's discuss these three stages in their relationship to the losses you and other members of your family are experiencing.

■ *The first stage of grief: an "urge to recover the lost object"*

When we first experience a loss, there is a sense of shock and numbness. Do you remember the first time you heard that your parents were getting a divorce, or when you first heard about the death of someone close to you? What was your reaction? Did you feel like you couldn't breathe, or that events were going on around you but you weren't aware of them? Did you then blank out some of the day's events and feel numb? These are reactions associated with feelings of denial and isolation.

Denial can greatly affect a blended family. One couple married after the death of the husband's wife, being utterly convinced that God had brought them together to raise both sets of children. They believed they would be the 'happily ever after' family. They were in total denial that they or their children needed time to grieve before the new family began. The husband was abandoned early in life by his father and so was extremely afraid of feeling the grief of his first wife's death. He, in particular, needed time to grieve his loss. Many people counseled the couple to allow time for their pain to heal, but they were determined to go ahead with the marriage immediately. The results were devastating for their family.

Denial does have a purpose, in that it helps the individual cope with the initial loss and defend himself against what will follow. The isolation is a kind of emotional cocoon, where one gains added strength and emerges with the ability to manage the new stress in life.

After this period of numbness, there is a great search for the person or persons who have been lost. We cannot believe they are gone, and we speak and act as if they are still present in our lives. At times this is even more difficult in the blended family because the person has not died but is not in our lives in the way we would wish.

This stage is accompanied, Bowlby points out, by weeping and anger—weeping for the person lost and anger at the person for going away. We weep for the people we cannot retrieve in the same roles as they were to us before. It really is like that first cry of the child who has been separated from his mother. Blended families have reported their children weeping in this inconsolable manner.

When the lost person cannot be retrieved, anger spills over into the blended family. The couple getting married is blamed for ruining the fantasy of the original family coming together again. This anger, resentment, and envy must be expressed. And most of the time, it will be directed at members of the new family.

People going through this anger stage of grief often ask themselves, "Why did this happen to me?" Often family and friends have trouble coping with a person in this stage because that person will lash out for no apparent reason; he is angry at everything and everybody. He is angry at the person who left him, yet also afraid of the intense anger coursing through him. Children especially fear that their anger could cause something bad to happen to a loved one.

At times like this, it is important to realize that the grieving person is not lashing out at you but at the loss; as a member of the new family, you trigger (remind him or her of) that loss. Attempts must be made to respect the person, despite the behavior, and try to understand the source of pain. This is where interpretations, which were discussed in previous chapters, can be very important. The angriest person really is feeling the most desperate about handling the loss.

Anger at God is another manifestation of this stage of grieving. Some people may suppress these feelings due to their strict religious beliefs, but others question those beliefs after experiencing a loss. Confronting a faith that seemed to have all the answers is common during this phase.

The degree to which we have handled our own losses will determine the way in which we can tolerate someone in our new family going through the anger stage. More than one person in the family may be going through this stage at a time. No wonder blended families can be such a powder keg!

The degree to which we can admit our own destructive impulses of anger and aggression will determine how well we can handle others expressing their rage at losing members of their previous families. As has been stated before, anger that has gone unresolved since childhood plays an important part in this stage of the grieving process.

What helps during this stage?

- Being supportive and respectful of the person even if his or her behavior is irrational at times.

- Coming to terms with our own views of loss and the grieving we still have to do.

- Encouraging mourners to talk about their anger, as opposed to acting it out.

- Trying to broaden our perspective and/or faith to include this experience of loss, and encouraging others do the same, in their own way.

A five-year-old girl had just become part of a blended family that included her father and stepmother. Her mother had abandoned the family several years before. At first she had been calm, although in looking back the parents said they did feel she had been in shock. Eventually her behavior changed and she began to throw terrible temper tantrums before bed, screaming, "I hate you" and kicking if either parent tried to get close enough to comfort her. She was losing sleep and becoming more and more unmanageable.

The parents went out and bought some storybooks on grieving, which they read to her. They asked her if she was angry that her mother was gone, and she confirmed this by saying she wished her mother was dead if she wasn't going to visit. She later revealed her immense guilt for having said such things and expressed fear that her mother would die and she wouldn't know. The parents then got her a Bo-Bo punching doll that she could hit when she was very angry. They would rock her before and after her bouts of anger, and when she threw tantrums they would sit as close to her as they could, speaking softly or playing music. It took some time, but she was able to stop the tantrums and talk more about her sadness at her loss.

Helping a person come to terms with losing a loved one cannot be rushed, and people cannot be forced to move to the next stage before they are able to handle the next step in the grieving process.

There are two ways of handling people when they are in this first stage of grieving.

Help break the isolation. People who are still in search of a loved one tend to isolate themselves emotionally and physically. It is important that other family members—particularly the adults—do not withdraw their support just because the person grieving does not take their advice or appear to be affected by their attempts at help. Many times we allow people to isolate themselves, not wanting to intrude on them, when staying away only reinforces their feelings of being lost and not belonging. Helping the person who is grieving to feel supported will help him or her move on to the next stage of grieving.

The goal for the grieving process is to integrate the memories and positive feelings so that grieving persons feel that they have the lost people with them even though those people have died or are no longer close to them. I call this "finding a new home for the person you have lost."

This does *not* mean that you accommodate someone remaining in a world of fantasy. You may still offer your opinion, especially if you see them headed in a dangerous direction.

One teen who was grieving over the loss of a home life with his father and former family would spend hours in his room, refusing to speak to his stepfamily. They allowed him privacy but told him that they cared for him and wanted him to spend time with the family. Each member made daily attempts to connect with him, even though he was not cooperative. They did not judge him for his behavior but did point out that what he was going through was a result of his grieving for his previous family.

Nurture those who are in grief. The person beginning the grieving process has been through a great shock and needs care. Consider your reaction to a person who has just found out they have terminal cancer or a person who has just lost a loved one. You would be very caring and understanding of his or her behavior. Many times we are not as understanding if someone in our family has just lost their family because we do not want to be reminded of our grief either. This especially applies to children who tend to act out their grief by becoming sullen and withdrawn or worse.

We must look for behavior that indicates grieving and then respond in a nurturing way that does not permit the person to become isolated.

■ *The second stage of grief: "disorganization"*

In this second stage of mourning, Bowlby points out there are similarities to depression in that there is great despair and hopelessness. The person grieving has given up his search for the loved one and feels a sense of disintegration of the soul.

When we finally realize that the person we have lost is not coming back to live with us and let us be a family the way we were before, depression sets in. Sometimes the person who has been lost is not coming back at all due to death or abandonment. Abandonment is in some ways more difficult to deal with because there is always a shred of possibility that the person will come back.

During this stage, the grieving person may feel like a lost child. He or she is clearly disoriented and, in some respects, does not care. When we do not see any meaning to life, it becomes difficult to organize the details of an average day, let alone life in general.

This is very difficult for the blended family because the husband and wife are wanting to get on with the new family, yet they have someone who requires constant care. Bowlby points out that some therapists treat this as regular depression, which generally it is not. If the person is despairing of his or her own self-worth, then it is depression based on earlier deprivations.

Many times, we are afraid to let other family members express their anxieties and sadness. Instead we try to encourage the person to get on with life and be happy. Families need to know that a person cannot experience relief from the sadness and "get on with life" until the grief is expressed and processed.

In this period of letting go of losses and preparing for the future, we can help family members by sharing their sadness and encouraging them to talk about how they feel. Nudge those who grieve to think about what they need. They need to understand that they are not abandoning a person by letting go. But they must finish saying good-bye to their loved one. Then they can find a new place for their memories and begin to join the new family.

I lost my grandfather, to whom I had been very close, when I was a young teenager. It has helped me in my grief to have pictures and belongings of his at times of sadness to comfort me and remind me of all he gave me during his life.

■ The third stage of grief: "reorganization"

Bowlby states that this is a period of shifting the place of the loved ones from outside in our external world to internalizing what they gave us and finding a new place for them within ourselves. What this means is, although the loved one is no longer with us physically (a parent dies or no longer lives in the same house), he or she is still a vital part of our lives—through our memories and what our time together has taught us.

This is, in fact, what the blended family is trying to do, isn't it? Everyone's role has been changed. We do not live with some of the people we used to. Some have died or abandoned us. Others we will only see on weekends or holidays. There is a period of reorganizing these roles and coming to accept them as part of our lives.

Acceptance is not a return to happiness, where the loss is no longer felt or mentioned but rather a willingness to say good-bye to a role we played with the person and develop a new role with him or her. Realizing that loved ones will always be a part of our lives, we will continue to hold onto the blessings and scars of that lost relationship.

The grieving person may need help in identifying those things that will offer the most comfort and solace. They need to identify what comforts them and what assistance they need from you to reestablish their lives.

This may be a quiet, internal time. There is a certain peace and dignity that people experience when they are finally able to say good-bye to what they have hoped for and lost. There may be less talk and fewer outward signs during this stage.

We must emphasize here that acceptance comes in all shapes and sizes. Some people pretend that the lost person never existed instead of coming to terms with a new way of perceiving the lost individual. Acceptance does not minimize the tragedy of the loss but allows people to continue their lives with peace and dignity.

The way we handle loss has a lot to do with our earlier childhood experiences and the degree of consistent nurturing we received. If there were problems and losses, this reorganization and acceptance will be more difficult. While we are in pain we tend to go back to early experiences and repeat those formative behaviors.

One final note: These stages do not necessarily follow one after the other, but can be experienced in combination with each other. People can travel back and forth between the various stages, as events and experiences trigger each other and bring forth memories of the past.

Differences in Grieving

The ways in which stages of grief are expressed depend on several factors.

■ *The relationship of the mourner to the person lost*

Even though people grow up in the same families, they are not all equally close. One family member may be able to go through the grieving process with less trauma, but that does not mean that another person in the family should be expected to grieve in the same way. Also, a person in the family who shared more *conflict* with the lost person may have more to deal with than those who were not as involved.

■ *The age of the person who grieves*

Certain developmental phases—such as puberty—already make heavy demands on the body and emotions; the added burden of grief is all the more difficult to process at such a time. Children who are too young to be verbally articulate will of course need to express what they are experiencing in ways other than heart-to-heart talks, and adults may have to be more creative in the ways they help small children.

A younger child has less resources to draw from because his ego structure is not developed enough to easily tolerate pain. ("Ego structure" here refers to the person's core personality.) A younger child thus responds to loss by regressing to a younger age, sometimes with a good deal of aggression.

An older child, age ten and on, is more likely to respond to loss and grief as an adult would. His ego is usually more fully developed than a younger child's, thereby lessening the chances of him blaming himself or others for the loss. Having more experiences of the world than his younger counterparts, the older child tends to be more flexible when viewing his grief. At the same time, some experts argue that the older child, especially the adolescent, becomes more fragile due to the stresses of this particular developmental stage.

■ *The person's psychological history and make-up*
The more loss or trauma a person has experienced as a child, the more affected that individual's ego development will be, and the more vulnerable he or she will be to trauma, even when grown.

What has transpired in any child's life prior to the loss is significant in helping or detracting from his ability to cope with the loss. For example, a mother of two had suffered a long bout with cancer prior to her death, thereby preventing her from caring for her children for many months. The children suffered the loss of their mother long before she died, and that affected their psychological development, making it much more difficult for them to attach to their stepmother when their father remarried.

Children especially need the opportunity to deal with grief in their own way and make restitution in their lives. We will talk about this more extensively later in the chapter, but it involves finding another "love object" (a person to give nurturance in a new way at this time in life) so that they have some solace. This should be the goal of the new family.

Unresolved Grief

When a person has been unable to grieve or to resolve grief, there is a range of symptoms that may occur. Some of these could be due to other problems, but they are an indication of unresolved grief and should be investigated further to help the person work through loss.

When a child is abandoned by a parent, whether in infancy or early childhood, there tend to be symptoms of heightened self-interest, aggression (especially toward oneself), loss of self-esteem, and fantasies of an ultimate rescuer. In addition, somatic symptoms may arise from this abandonment, either in later development or in adulthood. *Somatic symptoms* are real physical symptoms, often gastrointestinal in nature, for which no physical cause can be found. For example, colitis may be experienced more frequently in people who have been abandoned earlier in their lives, either physically or emotionally, although that is not to say that everyone with this disorder suffers from this type of deprivation.

Withdrawal, hatred, rage, depression, and hopelessness leading to despair are also indications that a person still has some grieving to do.

A teenage girl came into therapy because of her uncontrollable fits of rage. She would lose her temper, swear, hit things, and generally strike out at the slightest provocation. She had not known her father since he had abandoned the family when she was very small, and she felt equally abandoned by her alcoholic mother, who would tell the girl awful things about the father during her drinking bouts. In many cases, a parent's unresolved grief triggers the same reaction in the children.

Patterns of Regression

People in the throes of grief do *regress* into a more vulnerable and less functional emotional state: that is, they seem to move *backward* developmentally (e.g. a six-year-old suddenly begins to suck his thumb again, something he hasn't done since he was four). Some of these feelings originate in a fear of death. We all fear annihilation of our person, even if our faith sustains us. In the blended family there has been so much loss that it triggers our most fundamental fears of never belonging or being loved.

The two most basic emotional needs are to be loved and to belong. When threatened, people tend to feel that at least a part of them has been killed off, thus resulting in the fear of death. Obviously, the more abandonment, the more fear of death, which manifests itself in anxiety attacks and phobias.

Most people, children in particular, deal with this fear by using "projection." *Projection,* simply put, is seeing your feelings in someone else, or blaming another person for something that you experience internally. I see a lot of this at the children's home where I work. These children experienced deprivation and abuse in their families. Fights are constantly breaking out due to the attempt to blame someone else. Because their own feelings are so damaged, they are overwhelmed with grief at their loss. The anxiety of the loss is so high that they attempt to give that pain to someone else by blaming that person for wrongful behavior.

Denise and Haley, the daughters from our family story, both had trouble with projection as they worked through their grief. Haley, especially, was very angry at being part of a new family so late in her life, and so she projected her rage onto Denise, blaming her for absolutely everything that went wrong. Her parents did not escape her wrath either. She blamed them for caring more for Denise than for her, and for showing marked favoritism. In this way, Haley did not have to deal with her grief and anxiety about losing her new family after she went back to school. The great disadvantage of postponing her feelings was that she lost the opportunity to become closer to the household.

What is a parent to do with such conflict and pain? I'll sound like a broken record when I say, "Talk about it," but the principle still applies. Realizing that the person is really hurting over the deeper issues of grief, longing for love and belonging when he is blowing off steam and blaming others, is helpful in preventing reprisals and an escalation of anger in the family.

Restitution

This chapter has dealt extensively with the subject of loss, but now it is time to focus on *restitution,* the help for grieving. Restitution here refers to the making right of our lives, i.e., coming to peace with ourselves and others. Bowlby's stages illustrated that there is a natural progression in the grieving process—most people will eventually work their way through and find resolution. But there are ways in which a blended family can help its members through this process—all the way to its completion.

When a blended family first comes together there is a tremendous amount of hostility under the surface due to the losses all have experienced. If the family can see one of its first tasks as absorbing some of this hostility, the grieving can take place, and then the desired bonding can proceed.

This sounds frightening, and it is! But you who are parents may have already done this when your children were very young. Have you ever had your overtired toddler scream, carry on, and even strike out at you? Your response was to scoop him up, talk quietly, and put him to bed for a much-desired nap. You were absorbing his hostility. Why? Because you were a permissive parent and didn't set limits? No, because you knew the child had reached the limit of what he could tolerate, and you were assuming your role as parent by lending your strength to a tired child rather than punishing him for being crabby. This is what has to happen in a blended family.

The children especially feel that they have lost their families, the objects of their love, and at least one of their parents. They usually have great spurts of anger, which must be communicated before they can successfully transfer their affection to their current family. The blended family's job is to become a substitute for the original family, while keeping the importance of the original parent intact. Not an easy job! The substitution acts as a shock absorber, protecting each family member against his own self-destructive aggression and providing a place of belonging and love.

How does a family absorb the hostility of its members and continue on? Faith is one way in which restitution can take place. The two most important tasks for the family are to provide a sense of continuity in life and to help each individual feel cherished in the face of death and abandonment. The family cannot provide these things without outside help but must realize that a sense of belonging and being cared for goes beyond their physical being.

There are those who state that we "create" our Creator because of our inner needs. But others propose that the inner need exists for ultimate belonging to a Higher Being because it was created by God as part of our nature. The Creator wanted for us to know some sense of ultimate belonging and love, knowing there would be more pain and sorrow than we could bear. In reaching out for faith, we connect with this unconditional love. We can then communicate it more effectively to our families.

In Genesis, the first book of the Bible, we are given a prime example of a blended family in the story of Jacob, who unknowingly married Leah and later her sister, Rachel. The two sisters were in fierce competition over giving birth, but Rachel proved to be barren. She gave Jacob her handmaid to have children by, and then Leah followed suit by offering her maid. At last Rachel herself gave birth, but by that time there were twelve sons and four mothers! The hostility that followed spanned nations and many generations. However, through all the pain, anger, and loss there remained a great faith in God and a sense of purpose that helped solidify Israel as a nation. This is an example of restitution—substance out of pain.

The goal of the blended family is to provide a place for each person in the family and to assist him or her in grieving so that the family may bond and find a sense of equilibrium. If the family can provide for as many needs as possible, then each member can become a complete and mature individual, continuing life with a sense of peace and dignity. In short, members of the family become new love objects to one another.

6
What Are the Children
Going Through?
Understanding Children and Their Feelings

T wo little red-haired, green-eyed children sat looking at me apprehensively in my waiting room. Their mother had died a year ago from a long battle with lung disease. The girl, Agnes, was six, and the boy, Craig, was ten. Shortly after their mother's death, their father, Ron, decided to remarry. Sue was divorced for three years with a girl of her own, age four. The parents decided to move into Sue's home. Both Sue and Ron were very religious and believed that God would work everything out.

Agnes was in a learning disabilities class at school due to her reading problems. Craig was brought for therapy because of his uncontrolled aggressive behavior characterized by swearing, hitting, and breaking Sue's possessions. Sue's four-year-old initially had been "the angel" of the family but was now acting angry.

The parents were concerned about the children's behavior and sensed that the children had not gotten over the death of their mother. Ron and Sue conveyed a clear message from the beginning that the children were not acceptable the way they were, and needed to be "fixed" by the therapist.

When asked what they wanted from counseling and what they would like their family to be like, Agnes piped up brightly

87

and said, "One big, happy family." When I talked to Agnes and Craig separately, it was obvious that no one had ever talked to them about their mother's funeral. They had been through the whole process and no one had explained what had happened. I realized this when Agnes drew a picture of a black coffin on top of what looked like a red fire. When I asked her what the picture was about, she responded sadly, "This is the box they put my mother in." She did not even know what the coffin was called, what the service was for, and no one had explained what takes place at a funeral. She had no belongings or pictures of her mother.

We talked for a long time about what had happened at the funeral. We talked about the visitation, about taking the casket to the front of the church before the funeral, and about her mom being in heaven, which was the family belief. We also talked about how Agnes might be very sad and angry for a while till she finished grieving for her mom.

Craig, on the other hand, did not want to talk about what had happened at all. He had recurrent severe colds and frequent accidents. His drawings were all in black and were done very hurriedly. He would not tell me much about their content or his feelings about these pictures. He would not admit to or talk with me about his aggressive behavior at home or at school. He was also in the habit of leaving the house for long periods without telling anyone where he was going. He portrayed himself as tough, belligerent, and uncooperative. But inside his heart was broken.

When I brought up the possibility that he missed his mother very much and was sad and angry especially about the new marriage of his dad so soon after the death of his mother, tears formed in his eyes, but he refused to let them fall.

With coaching, Sue and Ron attempted to help Ron's children grieve for their mother. They gave them pictures of their mother and let the children choose to keep some of her things. Sue and Ron showed them keepsakes their mother had kept of them, i.e. baby curls, artwork, and the like. Sue talked and prayed with the children at night. But when there were difficult or emotional times, Ron could not bring himself to speak with the children. He could be present while Sue talked, but could not talk or spend time alone with them. His grief was still too fresh.

After the lull in the storm, things started to boil again. Both of Ron's children became disrespectful to Sue. Both started swearing and were deliberate in pointing out to her that she was not their real mother and she could not tell them what to do. Ron would punish them but could not participate in setting up new family guidelines. Craig started to run away, Agnes was kicked out of school several times, and both Craig and Agnes hit and teased Sue's daughter.

Family conferences with Sue and Ron revealed that no guidelines had been enforced on a regular basis with Ron's children, especially during the mother's illness, when she had been unable to care for them.

Unfortunately, the family was not willing to stay in treatment. They had hoped for a quick fix, perhaps to avoid the painful and difficult work involved in mourning and healing. ■

We must find the inner workings of children's problems if we are to meet their needs at this crucial time of change in a new family. Children are torn between both hopes and fears about fitting into a new family structure. The long-term parenting skills you learn will be an added benefit as the family begins to become more integrated.

Some of the issues at the heart of children's feelings are false expectations, fantasies, divided loyalties, attachment, loss, anger, resentment, fear, and loss of self-esteem.

False Expectations

The family's false expectations affected each of the children in the above example, possibly hindering them from grieving, from identifying the parent's roles in the family, and from finding their places in the family. *False expectations* here are being defined as any wish or desire that is not realistic but is believed by or imposed on the new emerging family. These expectations do have a valid side to them in that they indicate to the observant parent a symbol or sign of what the child's deeper needs are and what the child is struggling to achieve.

■ *Everybody's happy*

What Agnes said about her family being "One big, happy family" indicates one of the major false expectations that children bring into a blended family. Agnes thought that everyone would be happy to be joining this family, when in fact underneath she had many unresolved issues to be worked on that had remained uninvestigated. Children hold the fantasy of a happy family in order to deal with the breakup of the previous family.

■ *New kind of permanence*

Children have a difficult time understanding different degrees of permanence. Parents need to emphasize that brothers and sisters are still related, even though they are not living together. The same applies to the biological parent not living with the child, especially if that parent is absent from visitation.

■ *It's my fault*

Children, especially in times of stress, see things that happen as a direct result of their actions or because they are around when the event happened. They may see life's happenings from the vantage point of omnipotence or from a point of great helplessness, depending on the situation. Craig's violent behavior in the family story was the result of his belief that his bad behavior was responsible for his mother's death; he had feelings of omnipotence—that he could have been so powerful to have killed his mother. What this kind of expectation means is that the child does not feel there is a reliable adult in his life who can help manage these out-of-control feelings.

Very young children go through this powerful/powerless stage as a normal part of their development. This is heightened with the formation of the new family. An older child stuck at this stage may indicate that the child did not get his needs met at a much earlier stage of development. Going back to meet some of those early bonding needs may be key during the blending process.

One teenage girl sought older boys to be with after her parents' marriage broke up. Her behavior represented a seeking for the love and affection she missed during that traumatic time.

■ All we need is love

Another common expectation, held by parents as well as children, is that the love and caring of the new family automatically will make up for the losses the children have experienced. A related expectation holds that children do not have to go through a grieving process before attaching to the new parent and family. Both beliefs are false and very damaging to children, and they will sabotage the beginning of the new family. Studies about these problems indicate, as does the family in our example, that *if children have not grieved or been able to take time to let go emotionally of the previous family structure, they are unable to form new relationships that will be satisfactory.*

In order for the children to attach to another adult, they must first work through their grief. The new relationship will also bring back the grieving process for a time, so there must be a sufficient period of adjustment. The parents must educate themselves about the grief process, and it is up to them to provide a safe, supportive environment in which the children can work through their pain.

■ *What parents can do*

Learn to interpret children's symbolic "language." Children speak a particular language when it comes to their feelings. They communicate to us through symbols, because their verbal skills are not developed at an adult level. Those of us who care for children must learn what these symbols mean in order to understand what the children are trying to tell us. These symbols are often evident in art and behavior. If we can interpret them correctly, we can help our children work through many difficult feelings. They will feel understood, and attachment to the new family can begin.

In the family story, both Agnes's and Craig's art showed how they were grieving. Agnes's coffin on fire and Craig's drawing all in black were strong indicators of the distress they were experiencing—feelings they were unable to express in other ways.

Be in touch with your own false expectations. We must not contribute to our children's false expectations by being out of touch with our own. If we show inappropriate disapproval over our children because they are still in grief when we think they should be happy or cooperative, we demonstrate false expectations to them and burden them unfairly. But if our children see us being honest about our own difficulties and learn from our attitudes that the changes in the family take time, they can let go of damaging expectations. We must be aware of the expectations members of our family may have and try to identify them correctly.

Explain—as often as necessary—what is happening in the family. We must talk, talk, talk to our children, explaining to them the grieving process and the many changes that they have difficulty understanding on their own. We need to ask them what they would like to see happen, get their input on the transition, and be willing to adjust our timetable accordingly. We must ask them what they expect and need from the new family. We must help them verbalize their fears. An overriding atmosphere of "get with the program" and enforced happiness does not produce a family and denies children their place in it.

Fantasies

What imaginary wishes do you see your children having? What fantasies do you remember having as a child? Children hold on to fantasies for security and to fulfill wishes that do not come true in everyday life.

Fantasies are defense mechanisms that help us deal with unpleasurable experiences. They are, in effect, stories that we tell ourselves to help us deal with parts of life that are too difficult for us. Because they are not yet as sophisticated as are adults, children are more spontaneous and transparent with their fantasies. Their personalities are not yet fully developed to handle certain traumas, so fantasies are a temporary help. Children of blended families have experienced a great deal of stress both prior to and during the formation of the new family system, so fantasies enable them to deal with all these changes.

■ *Types of fantasies*

Reunited parents. One of the most common wishful fantasies for children of divorce is that their parents will get back together again. The remarriage puts an abrupt end to this fantasy and often leaves the child disillusioned, blaming himself, and feeling there is no hope.

Denial. Many children may deny the real separation of the divorced couple. The parent furthers the denial by telling the child that the parent who is not living with the family is just away on a trip. If the custodial parent is overwhelmed by the separation, this parent's disturbance may contribute to the child's denial. I have seen some parents contribute to the denial of their children by telling them for years that they are praying that God will bring the ex-spouse back into the relationship. Many of these practices reinforce the denial for children and make it much more difficult for them to grieve and bond with the new family.

The ideal parent. To overcome their helplessness during the breakup of the original family and during the formation of the blended family, children may choose one parent to be the "ideal" parent. Usually they choose the one who is lost to them to be positive and focus their negative feelings onto a current parent, usually the stepparent. When Craig said to Sue, "You are not my mom," he was making her the "bad mom" that had abandoned him by death.

One boy made a hero out of his father after his parents divorced. According to the boy, the mother who had custody was to blame for driving the father away even though he had been somewhat threatening in the home. The mother saw the child's action as a sign that she was the only person he felt would not go away and therefore he felt comfortable directing his anger at her. When she was able to reflect this to him, telling him she was willing to take his anger, he was able to settle down a bit and concentrate more on his schoolwork. He gained success and some self-esteem and was less combative at home and after visits with the father. Parents need to realize that a child may devalue one parent and idealize the other in order to cope with their devastating vulnerability created by the separation and loss.

Normally, preschool children fantasize freely due to their tendency to think magically. Since their reasoning ability is not fully developed, they make up stories to deal with situations they find themselves in, especially stressful ones or ones that have not been adequately explained to them. Parents of children this age should consider this normal and expect fantasizing to increase as the new family forms. With older children, regression to fantasy is a sign of stress. Parents can discuss the fantasies with their children to determine what feelings are being manifested in the fantasies. Knowing how your children feel will then guide your interventions to help your children fit into the family setting.

A little girl whose father had abandoned the family fantasized about three imaginary sisters. One was bad, one was good, and one took care of her and the other two imaginary sisters. When she was able to talk about how confused and sad she was over her father leaving and how she was not to blame, the sisters vanished as magically as they had appeared.

What if ... ? Subconscious fantasizing about what the previous marriage could have been like if it had lasted occurs in adults as well as children. Children are more prone to this fantasy through their play and drawing, thus admitting to the fantasy. Parents need to acknowledge all fantasies of the child as wishes and sadness surrounding the issues of loss and separation.

Family secrets contribute to children's unhealthy fantasies. In the family story, the guilt both parents felt inhibited them from talking realistically with the children about their current pain. The telling of secrets must be handled with extreme care and probably with the guidance of a therapist, a pastor, or trusted friend. Leaving secrets unattended is to wait for a time bomb to go off in an already fragile situation.

Children, no matter what their age, see discovered secrets as lies told them by their parents. Secrets dealing with birth information, alcohol abuse, and family heritage are especially difficult, and their telling should be guided by a professional. There is no correct way to deal with family secrets, except that there should be no deceptions, and secrets must be dealt with honestly, which usually requires outside help. *Secrets will come out in some way* if not addressed.

Children's fantasies must be acknowledged as their way of dealing with fears and anxieties about the new family and the memories of the old one. Fantasies and memories protect children from being overwhelmed, and therefore sometimes should be left intact until the child is better able to deal with reality. I sometimes say to children, "I know you have to believe that for right now."

Children who have been ridiculed or unaccepted for their secret wishes often turn to self-harm (i.e., suicidal thoughts or gestures; rage attacks, distortion of reality, head banging, biting, pulling out hair, to name a few) as a way of handling their anxieties. The solution for parents is to talk about what the child wishes or fears and to interpret the play and acting out behavior as signals for help in coping with overwhelming feelings. *When feelings of self-harm are involved, parents should seek professional help immediately.*

Divided Loyalties

What are divided loyalties? Children feel they are betraying the original family when they go with the new family, especially if they have positive feelings for the stepparent or even the biological parent they are living with. Feelings of disloyalty exist for children whether they are actually living with the family or are having regular custody visits. These feelings can also apply to the siblings children have left behind. When children experience pleasure, enjoying the company of the new stepsiblings, they may feel disloyal to the siblings from whom they are separated. Wanting to be with the stepfamily or liking the stepparent and still wanting a relationship with the biological parent can be very confusing and upsetting for children. Adults find it difficult to realize that we can have two opposing feelings about something or someone. But it is even more difficult for children, who have fewer developmental resources and life experiences to support them in their conflict.

■ *What aggravates divided loyalties?*

Denial. Some children deny the permanence of the breakup between their parents of origin.

Waiting for absent parents. Some children are in a waiting pattern, wanting to resume a role with the biological parent and feeling it would be disloyal if they were to attach to a new adult in that same role. Waiting appears more frequently with children who have lost a parent through death or where the noncustodial parent does not visit.

Parent's lack of resolution. Children may become confused if the parent they live with has not broken emotional ties with the ex-spouse. Parents can tell what the issues are in the family system by the child's "acting-out" behavior. Children act as mirrors to our own unfinished business because we are their models. This is illustrated in the family story with Agnes and Craig. The father had not grieved for his previous wife, so the children did not feel permission to express their sorrow for her either.

Parents blaming each other. When the ex-spouse is consistently blamed, a child is put in tremendous conflict. The child fears rejection and disapproval from the parent he lives with but still wants to maintain a relationship with his other parent. If the child has to give up the proper attachment to either parent, he then may act out negatively, grieving the loss of that parent.

Judgment of grandparents. Grandparents may add fuel to the fire if they are critical or unaccepting of the new relationships. Parents, especially in the first year of the blended family, must monitor and instruct other relatives on how to approach the children, to protect them from the pressure of having to take sides in the family conflict. At the same time, the new family needs to make an effort to stay in contact with extended family who are significant to the children.

Relationships with new parents. If the child is living with the parent he feels most comfortable with, there may not be as many problems with divided loyalties because there is more a feeling of choice. But when the child begins to form a new relationship with the stepparent, the issues of divided loyalties may resurface.

Teenagers also have trouble with divided loyalties because they may have spent much more time in the original family and their goal developmentally is to separate from their family, trying on more adult roles. To have to make an emotional commitment at this time presents them with a great deal of confusion because they still want to be part of a family, but they want to venture off to begin their adulthood as well.

■ *How can parents work with divided loyalties?*

Don't pressure your children. Pressure should not be placed on a child to accept the new relationships before he or she is ready. The stepparent may get very mixed messages for a while, one minute having a loving, engaging child and the next a hostile, provocative one. This is an indication that the child is trying to work out mixed feelings.

Help children interpret their own emotions. Interpret these feelings for the child to help him feel validated in these mixed emotions. The message the new parent wants to give is: "I will be here for you, but I realize it will take you some time to sort this all out. I am in no way wanting to take the place of your parents, but I do want to support and care for you in any way I can. I want to have the kind of relationship that is acceptable to both of us and that we can work out together."

Encourage children to become their own persons. Look for their qualities and reflect and praise them. "I noticed you work really well with your hands. That bracelet you made the other day is beautiful."

Don't expect your children to meet all your needs. The child does not exist to meet the parent's needs; the parent is to care for the child.

Give children freedom in choosing their relationships. Allow them to form the attachments they are comfortable with in their own way and at their own pace. Allow them to choose who they bond with first in the family.

Christ said, "Let the children come to me, and do not hinder them; for to such belongs the kingdom of God" (Mark 10:14). He knew the importance of listening to children. When the disciples were shooing the children away, Christ brought the children back to be cared for, not considering the adults' agenda more important than the children's.

Attachment

We devoted all of chapter 4 to attachment, but let's talk about it here as it affects children during this blending period of their lives.

A very small child, under two years of age, has the best chance of attaching to the stepparent because of the degree of care still necessary and the early onset of the relationship. Obviously, the older the child and the more separations the child has had, the more difficult will be the attempts to attach. Passage of time and the child having your permission to work through old conflicts are both keys to enabling the child to form a relationship with the stepparent and accept the new family. Each child has his own inner timetable and reacts differently to the family history. When I see a child in my practice, I obtain information about her birth and early development. This gives me insight into the mother/child relationship and can help to explain why the child develops problems at later stages in life.

Each child should be allowed to develop at his own rate, while the stepparent gives messages of support, nurturance, and unconditional acceptance. In order to compensate for the child's high level of anxiety, the biological parent in the family must increase bonding and support by spending more time with the child, listening to his concerns, and interpreting the feelings involved. The child must know that there is at least one parent of the original family that is supportive at this crucial time.

A colleague whose wife died several years ago is raising a daughter on his own. He has begun to go out with a woman with whom he is becoming more serious. His daughter is excited and has started calling this woman for advice. The father cautioned her that the woman is not her mom and that he does not know whether they will be together permanently. In talking with his daughter he is keeping an open dialogue and also protecting his daughter appropriately.

The child must also be given the clear message that she is not expected to have as close a relationship with the new family as to the original family. *Children should be able to choose the level of closeness in the family but should not be allowed to be destructive or hurtful to the stepparent.* This emotional bonding, stemming from the new parent's daily nurturance and understanding, earns the parent the right to intervene in a more in-depth fashion.

From the beginning, Sue (in our family story) was expecting the attachment level to be unrealistically high and, in fact, equal with that of the biological mother. No doubt this was based on her own need for a sense of belonging. Parents who project their own needs onto their children aggravate an already stressful period in the lives of the children.

■ *How parents can help with attachment issues*

Talk. Attachment can be discussed with children. Explain to them that you do not expect them to care for you right away but that you value them. You care for them no matter how they feel and want them to care about you in time.

101

The biological parent of the couple should also talk to the child about the details of the child's birth and how thrilled the parents were with the child's birth, if in fact this was the case.

Be prepared for them to test you to see if you mean what you say.

Find new ways of sharing your lives. One way of establishing a new family is to begin to create new traditions and activities. Simple celebrations in the course of daily and weekly events can set reassuring patterns for children and build with them a sense of belonging.

Loss

How did you feel when you lost a valued object? When you moved to a new home? When you lost a loved one? Even positive events that involve change can produce a sense of loss. Stepfamilies begin by dealing with loss because all the members of the new family have lost important members of their original families through death or divorce. As adults, we have learned to make substitutions or go on with our lives, but for children, loss is much more overwhelming and disrupting.

Many events in life represent loss to children: a move, birth of a sibling, illness or death of a parent, and divorce. The sense of loss is compounded for children if the loss is not recognized, appreciated, and talked about in the new family. For example, a man had not been told he was adopted as he was growing up. After discovering the secret in his adult life, he constantly viewed the world with suspicion, through a haze of betrayal.

We must again realize that children who have lost a primary parent, either through death or divorce, view life as no longer safe or secure, as they once believed it was. Children have difficulty seeing death as final, because they fear losing all control and being destroyed by the loss themselves. With divorce, children see the world as no longer permanent (i.e. if the family is not stable, then what else in life can be trusted?).

■ *What does the child need at a time of loss?*

Reassurance. At this point in time, repeated expressions of care and understanding are more important than anything else.

Acknowledgment. Sometimes children are too overwhelmed by all the changes in the family to acknowledge their worst fears. It is up to the parent to then acknowledge, for instance, that the child fears losing the other parent.

So involved in his own loss was the father, Ron, in our story, that he was unable to reassure his children of his presence; it was as if they had lost him, too.

Time to mourn. All of the literature indicates that children need to mourn longer than we realize, and we must give them that time. Get books to read on the stages of grieving and storybooks for your children *that you read and discuss with them!*

The number-one rule for a parent in these situations is to *see the children's behavior as a plea for support and care.* Keep in mind how difficult the divorce and remarriage have been for you. It is much more difficult for your children, who are not as experienced as you are at handling life's hard lessons; neither are they as equipped emotionally to deal with pain or make sense of their circumstances.

Parents need to help their children understand that they are not to blame for the death or divorce. The new relationship and family trigger feelings of guilt. The children feel they were unable to get their parents back together, or they were so bad they were responsible for the parent's death. Feelings of guilt keep coming back, especially in times of stress and sorrow.

As parents we try to spare our children from sadness and grief, but in doing so we rob them of moving on to the next stage in their lives and of accepting the new family. Many parents also have great ambivalence at dredging up old memories, but children need to talk and remember.

Anger

Anger and self-blame may serve to disguise children's feelings of hopelessness in recovering the lost parent. The process of letting go of a parent is so painful for children that they need a defense and so resort to direct hostility. Especially if their current needs are not being met and no one understands that they are experiencing extreme loss, the anger intensifies into rage.

One of the boys I see in therapy at the residential children's home was devastated because his mother had abandoned the family. He was sadly recounting that he had a dream about his mother coming to get him. Later in the day, I saw him on the playground shoving his brother angrily down on the ground. A childcare worker sent him to his room and to bed for the night. The child erupted into violent swearing, kicking, and biting, and had to be carried physically from the playground. It's too simplistic to say all this could have been avoided, but perhaps if his sadness at being abandoned by his mother had been explained as the source of his rage, it could have prevented his hostile action. He might even have felt comforted.

Limits need to be set, but when anger erupts, especially in a child who has experienced loss, it needs to be seen in the light of those losses and the child's feelings of inadequacy to deal with them.

There are several other triggers that cause the child to use anger as a defense to cope with loss. The child may actually be angry at the parent who has died or abandoned him, but he feels too guilty about expressing that anger verbally. So instead he directs the anger at the stepparent. The child may also feel he is to blame for the parent's death or divorce, so with anger and fits of rage he may try to break up the new couple.

The parents may be so traumatized by past losses and feelings of failure that they fear failure in the next relationship. In this instance, they are ready to blame all the family's woes on the child. The child then becomes the identified problem, when each member of the family needs to take a look at his feelings and the family dynamic as a whole. I usually see families during this stage, due to their fear of another failed relationship.

The angry child may be acting out what is happening in the family. In our family story, Craig believed his bad behavior caused the mother's death. The truth was that while the adults knew she was dying, they never told the children. The children had less time to prepare and grieve than the adults. The family secrets caused an immense amount of rage in the children. We assume children are weak where they are strong and strong where they are weak. We don't want them to be sad, yet we keep secrets that cause more damage in the long run.

Children take a longer time to achieve a sense of belonging in the new family. Until then, they feel like outsiders in their own family and experience feelings of exclusion, intrusion, and rejection, which result in anger and depression.

Children need reassurance that their feelings are normal and that the rest of the family feels a bit strange as well. It's possible to help children experience some special ways of belonging (e.g., having their choice of bedroom and decorating when possible). Parents must find out what makes them feel settled and then try to implement their wish. In the family story, the children were uprooted from their home without being consulted, and neither child was allowed to choose his or her room. This was one of the main contributing factors to Craig's destroying Sue's property. He felt he had no place of his own and had not only lost his mother, but his bed and all his other possessions.

Another source of the child's anger is the conflict caused by the bitter outpouring of the noncustodial parent against the new parent when the child visits. The child may be very attached to this parent and yet comes home and acts out all this anger that he has collected over the visit. The divided loyalty tears the child apart because his life feels like a war zone. As difficult as it may be, the biological parent must confront this issue openly with the child and ex-spouse.

The child needs to have permission to express his anger in a manner that is acceptable and agreed upon. Unacceptable behavior needs to be clearly defined. Above all, the child's feelings need to be interpreted as confusion and anger at the betrayal by both original parents. The ex-spouse needs to be talked to in a calm, rational manner about meeting the child's needs. The stepparent should not be involved directly in this. We must bear the burdens for our children and not expect them to play go-between for us. Otherwise, the anger can fester, repeat itself, and eventually turn into resentment.

Resentment

Resentment moves one step beyond anger but is related to it. *Resentment* in this context refers to anger that has been unattended to; issues that have been left unresolved create resentment. When a child has been unsuccessful in many attempts to get his needs met, he becomes deeply angry and hostile. Resentment is more prevalent in the teen and preteen years simply because there has been more time for the needs to go unresolved. The child feels his needs have not been considered and that he was not consulted or made a part of the family changes. The child also may feel that the moves were made too fast when he was not yet ready.

Resentment can also arise from all the changes over which the child has no control. Most of the changes in the child's life have been decided by the adults. In the family story, Sue was the one making all the decisions and then implementing them. Children resent discipline if it is carried out before the new attachment has formed. The biological parent needs to do the disciplining in the first few months until the children have become accustomed to the new parent. Resentment is greater if the ex-spouse was abusive, does not visit regularly, or is disruptive to the new family. Children have no control over such behavior from adults. *A parent's out-of-control behavior is one of the major causes of resentment in children, especially older ones.*

Physical symptoms such as headaches, stomachaches, chronic colds, flu, etc. can be an indication that the child has some deep-seated resentment. If the symptoms are frequent and have no physical explanation, a parent should certainly investigate further and even consider professional help. Craig's colds, for example, were a clear indication of his rage that was literally suffocating him.

■ *How then do we help resolve resentment?*

Interventions are crucial at this point so that the resentments will not progress into depression or delinquent behavior. Usually, the losses leading to resentment have not been resolved.

The parents need to admit that there is a problem and seek professional help if they cannot make successful interventions within a short period of time.

The key is to try to go back to where the problem started for the child. Ask, "When was the first time you felt like this? What was happening in the family then?"

Implementing the concept of forgiveness, both in your own life and with your children, helps the family to let go of bitterness and brings the family together. As parents, we must be willing to ask forgiveness from our children for putting them through this ordeal of the divorce or the remarriage. This is a difficult concept and should be done more in the context of searching your own conscience: for instance, when you feel you have been unfair, have caused pain, or have not considered the child's point of view. We need to help the child work through the resentment and let it go. In this way, the child can begin to restore self-esteem and self-value, and healing in the family relationships can begin.

Fear

■ *What does a child fear most?*

The new family will fall apart. Since the child's original perception of the family was one of eternal stability, the main fear from which many of the other fears stem is that this family will fall apart, too. Having had this stability shattered, the child is reluctant to believe again, in order not to be disappointed. The child is the most fragile link in the family structure because of the fear of abandonment that is triggered by his lost sense of security. A child is not able to care for and support himself in society. When the child has times of vulnerability and is worried about the fragility of the family relationships, he becomes very fearful.

Children may evidence these fears in all sorts of ways. They may cry or have a tantrum if they are younger; they may act out or become sullen if they are a bit older. Children, especially young children and adolescents, tend to express their anxieties in bodily symptoms.

They will not be able to see the parent they do not live with. If the family has moved to another town or state or if the visitation has been inconsistent, the fears are intensified. If children have observed conflict or abuse with the ex-spouse, they may be afraid to go to the visitation. In some cases the court will still force children to go into situations that are very frightening for them. At times such as this, the children may experience nightmares, bed-wetting, eating problems, and many other psychologically disturbing symptoms.

They will not fit into the new family. Children fear being rejected by the family altogether. They fear also that the noncustodial parent will reject them if they attach to the new family. Seeing other stepsiblings come and go on weekends makes them wonder when their turn will come to leave the family.

■ *How do we comfort children who are fearful?*
Some fears can be helped through reassurance and talking. More intense fears may require professional intervention, especially if the children are exhibiting physical symptoms, depression, or talking about harming themselves.

Verbalize the fear. It is helpful for the entire family to admit an awareness of the fear that things might not work out. Verbalized fear can be dealt with, while hidden fears increase problems for everyone in the family. The child is encouraged by example to speak his fears, and the parents can help him feel assured and protected because they know what the child is feeling.

Allow trust to grow. Parents should realize that the child's trust has been broken due to severed relationships in the previous family. It takes time and perseverance before the child can let go of the fears that his new family will break up. *The child should never be pressured with the question, "Don't you trust me?"* Trust comes in bits and pieces as the child becomes ready to invest in the new family.

Experience prayer. Prayer can be a great comfort for our children. Teaching children that they may pray for help and reassurance wherever they are, even if the parent is not around, is reassuring to them. A child may have questions about why God let the family break up; such a question has no easy answer, but this is a good time for children to learn that we can talk to God about everything. If they can see prayer as reassurance and affirmation of God's uncon-ditional love for them, this not only helps with the fear but promotes self-esteem and trust.

Loss of Self-Esteem

Self-esteem rests upon a feeling of being valued and loved, as well as being able to accomplish our goals in society. For the child the goal is to be able to live effec-tively and happily in the new family. When the child lives in a family atmosphere of affirmation, love, and communication, she develops a positive self-image. As parents we are responsible for the safeguarding of our children's growth and development; this encourages them to develop God-given talents and a strong identity. Many say that all we need is one significant adult to walk through life with us, to help us believe in ourselves.

The losses the child has experienced and the resulting emotions have been very damaging to the child's view of herself. She consequently feels she can't do things right. If there has been a great deal of conflict with overwhelming emotions at home, the parents may have been too preoccupied to tell the child how valued and loved she is.

■ *How do parents build self-esteem with their children?*

One of my colleagues recently adopted a baby, and when I was visiting one day, she put the child to bed. I was touched to hear her softly telling the almost-sleeping baby how glad she was that they had him, how he was part of their family, and how he was such a wonderful child. Love-and-valuing messages throughout our children's lives go a long way to heal the pain they have experienced. Such affirmation gives them energy and belief to make something beautiful out of their lives, despite loss and pain.

Environment also plays a large part in helping our children to value themselves in this stressful time. Studies show that children who come from blended families do better if they have other children who come from the same environment in their school, church, and neighborhood. Patricia Lutz, in her article on adolescence and stepfamilies, states that adolescents said they did not mind having a different last name from that of their family if there were others in their school that had the same experience.

I had two children in therapy who were from a single-parent family. The father did not visit at all, which contributed to the children's adjustment problems. They were the only children in their classes who did not have two parents at the PTA. They were also in a lower socioeconomic bracket than the rest of the children in their school. Although parents cannot just pick up and move in order to produce a conducive environment, they can make a special effort to involve their children with others of similar experience.

Taking children to support groups for blended families or other such functions can be crucial to building self-esteem. A child who feels good about himself will be able to adjust and integrate into the new family.

Building self-esteem is sort of like constructing a building; individual blocks eventually turn into a house. One of the key building blocks is positive memories. For children who have had a lot of damaging experiences, you can help them to talk about painful memories and to make positive ones. The new family is fragile, and so is the child's self-esteem. Creating positive memories through simple experiences and allowing the child choices in his life, where he had few choices before, is crucial.

For example, the child could come home from a stressful custody visit to a special time with the family, to his favorite meal, or to a favorite story. Creating positive memories goes a long way in establishing links the new family is building.

Affirmation and encouragement are the fuel that enables a child to function successfully in the new family. You may want to begin to consider the spiritual aspects of affirmation through learning to affirm God's love and positive spiritual messages that can be integrated into the child's life. Knowing the unconditional love of God on a daily basis can be a support during a period of grief and transition. Many families attempt to use religion to make the feelings go away, but the result is to chase the feelings into another playing field. With "true spirituality," as Francis Schaeffer called it, a personal relationship with God, we gain new strength and insight into our lives and a deeper knowledge of ourselves and the world around us. We need to teach our children to access God's spiritual power that is available to them and to see themselves and the world in a more accepting light.

Goals

Remember what it was like to be a child? Maybe if we adults remembered more about being a child we could relate in a more accepting way to our children. Our goal is to insure that every child in the family should feel valued and loved just for who he or she is. Each child should be aided in finding his or her place in the family.

Parents in blended families need to assist their children in:

- Expressing feelings of grief over the loss of original family

- Enabling them to work through those feelings of grief

- Starting to form new attachments through acceptance and affirmation

These goals are also accomplished through learning how to listen to your child, through providing support and reassurance as well as allowing yourself as the parent to hurt for the child and to share some of your pain with him. As a parent, learn to interpret the child's behavior so that when he acts out you can help him get to the root feelings.

From an early age, talk to your child about the goals she has for her life. What does she want for herself? Who does she want to be? What does she want to do with her life today, tomorrow, and when she's an adult? What are her goals in the new family, in school, in five years, later when she's grown up? In this way you establish your faith in her and show her that you are willing to stand by her throughout life. *You are not as interested in her good behavior as you are in her as a person!* Have you noticed how a child brightens in a group of adults when you ask her what grade she is in at school? You are treating her as an equal person.

Entering the world of children's feelings can be painful. But it's also rewarding as your children learn to trust you because you are committed to them and to the new family.

7
"Where Is My Other Mom (or Dad)?"

Parents without Custody

When members of a blended family come together they may not consider the effects of the ex-spouse's situation on the new family's development. In this chapter we will address some of the problems that families have when there is an uncooperative ex-spouse. We will also explore some of the custody issues that affect the blended family.

Our goal is to develop a co-parenting model by which the parents may share in the responsibilities of raising the children, even though they are no longer married. First, let's look at the feelings and experiences of the noncustodial parent.

Noncustodial Parents

Can you imagine what it would be like to lose one of your children? The noncustodial parent, many times the father, not only suffers the loss of his relationship with his spouse but also loses his home and children. This does not refer to the parents who have abandoned their families, displayed abusive behavior, or neglected child-support payments, but to the noncustodial parent who has lost much of his or her parent life in the process of the family breakup. For the purposes of this book *noncustodial parent* will refer to parents whose children do not live with them on a permanent basis.

FAMILY STORY

A

fter much marital unrest and his wife's eventual demand that they divorce, Ed decided to leave her and his three-year-old son. He was not only devastated by the loss of his son but concerned about how the divorce would affect the child. Ed had trouble functioning after he left his wife and tried to manage his grief by throwing himself into his work. The result was insomnia and uncontrollable crying spells. Chronic fatigue plagued him, even after waking from a good night's sleep. ■

The grief and sense of loss that noncustodial parents feel are overwhelming. They find themselves living in a different place, because the parent with the children is often the one who stays in the family home. Statistics show that the grieving process may take up to several years to complete. The parent who loses custody of the children suffers great deprivation from which, in a sense, there is no recovery.

Let's look at some of the emotional issues that noncustodial parents experience.

■ *Loneliness*

Noncustodial parents who are reading this book can probably identify with Ed. For those individuals working to form a blended family, it might be helpful to try to empathize with some of the feelings the ex-spouses may be experiencing. As we progress through these issues, see if you can put yourself in the place of the other person. What would it be like for you if you lost your children? What would you be feeling right now? How would all of this make you act?

Ed experienced feelings of utter loneliness that progressed into feelings of abandonment and total hopelessness. He demonstrated these feelings by staying late at work and not wanting to be alone in his apartment. His crying represented the feeling of being hopelessly alone in the world with no one to care for him and no one to care about. Loneliness can be debilitating. The worse you feel, the more inert you become. You cannot mobilize yourself to get out and meet people. Sometimes you even have difficulty participating in activities with the children you miss.

Many people do not know how to comfort themselves under normal circumstances, so in the throes of a family tragedy it is very difficult to think of ways to find comfort or raise self-esteem. Loneliness can be very hard on self-esteem and can cause great feelings of worthlessness. Finding ways to comfort oneself is important in avoiding immobilization. Again, we are not talking about repressing or pushing down emotions or making them go away. We want to feel the emotions, but we do not want them to get in the way of moving to the next step in our lives.

■ *Inadequacy*

Many parents who have lost their children in a custody fight feel inadequate—that had they been better parents, or tried harder with their spouses, or made more money, they could have saved their families. This could be called the "If only" syndrome: "If only I had done things differently, the situation might have been saved."

If the visits with the children do not go well, this distorted thinking is confirmed. Sometimes parents will overcompensate on visits in an attempt to make up for these feelings by taking the children everywhere and buying them everything—when the children just want to be with their parents.

Ed always had mixed feelings on the days he visited with his son. He was excited to see him and wanted to do as much as possible with him in the time they had together.

He also felt sad that he could not have his son with him all the time. When he would pick up his son, the child would cry for his mother. This made Ed think that his son did not want to be with him. When the boy cried at night, wet the bed, became ill, or would not eat, Ed grew frantic. At other times, he felt some indifference toward his son. He believed that his wife handled the child better than he could. There were times when he did not even feel like the child's real parent anymore, to the degree that he would return his son early if the situation became too stressful. ▪

What was Ed feeling?

How did Ed's feelings of inadequacy affect his behavior with his son?

Do you ever feel inadequate? When?

Ed assumed that his son cried because he did not want to be with him, when, in fact, the child was responding to the stress of the situation and not to Ed personally. The incident was not a judgment of Ed's care. When Ed was married to the child's mother, he had to travel extensively and was not as involved in the daily care of his son. Therefore, he was not as familiar with the child's routines and patterns, and he misinterpreted what may have been normal upsets.

At times, noncustodial parents abdicate the care of their children to other people, such as relatives or sitters, or bring the children home early because of their feelings of inadequacy. This only adds to the chaos, furthering the parent's sense of inadequacy, making the child feel rejected, and angering the ex-spouse.

Noncustodial parents need to give themselves positive messages and work on what would make them feel more prepared for the rigors of weekend parenting. After all, you can only go to the zoo so many times! Joining a support group of other noncustodial parents to problem-solve and understand what other parents go through might aid your self-esteem. Parenting classes could also prove beneficial. Sometimes sharing the feelings of loneliness and grief lightens the burden.

Some noncustodial parents feel ashamed of past actions, such as not visiting, not paying child support, or having someone else care for the children the entire time during visitation. Parents cannot give themselves encouraging messages if their behavior does not match what they are telling themselves. In order to take the next step, it is necessary to straighten out those actions, talk to the parties involved, and ask their forgiveness. Most of all, one must forgive oneself and one's ex-spouse for the breakup. This subject will be dealt with more extensively in the chapter on healing and forgiveness.

■ Managing visits

We saw how Ed had difficulty managing visits with his son. What are some of the emotions that trouble noncustodial parents? And what could make the visits a more positive experience for both parent and child?

119

■ *The bond has been broken.*

When people marry, they promise to love one another until their death. Children feel that their families will go on forever. When a family breaks up, everyone is devastated. There is no question that the bond that tied the family together has been broken. When there are visits between child and parent, especially in the beginning, it is extremely difficult for both parties. They feel estranged, hurt, and reminded that they are not in the same home anymore.

Talking to children about feelings of loss and grief is an excellent way to start the rebonding process. Even with small children, parents can read them books about divorce and have them draw pictures of how they feel. Parents can also share their own sadness about the family's breakup, thereby facilitating the healing process.

■ *Where is home?*

We all need a place that we can call home. Home is the place where we can be ourselves and relax. But divorce disrupts that environment. There is no longer a safe and comfortable place for the parents and the children.

How do you feel about where you live? How does it express who you are and what is important to you? How does it fit the needs of your children who visit? How do you feel when you are in your home?

The way we felt in our home growing up has a tremendous impact on the way we feel about finding a new home.

FAMILY STORY

Ed did not feel comfortable in the apartment he had selected. Procrastinating because of his inner conflicts, he had chosen hastily, picking a place close to the highway and near his work. He had left his wife and son with great difficulty, and the darkness of the one-bedroom apartment matched his mood.

Neither he nor his son liked staying at the apartment on their visits together, so they usually went to Ed's mother's home. She would cook for them, and she loved seeing her grandson. Ed always felt like a child himself when he went there and felt displaced once again. His son enjoyed his visits, but they did not have much time together when they were with his mother. When they would spend the night at Ed's apartment, they would have to bring everything over from his son's house and then lug it back again. ■

What emotions do you think Ed and his son were experiencing?

Ed was not proud of his home. He wasn't comfortable there. His story is an example of how unresolved feelings can affect one's ability to make decisions. Ed gave up part of his time alone with his son to his mother—because of his anxiety. Since he's still grieving the loss of his previous life, he didn't feel free to start his own life by getting settled with furniture, belongings, toys, and food for his son at his new place.

It's important to children that their environment express welcome and comfort. Then you can build a better relationship with them during this difficult time. And having a haven in which to rebuild life is crucial not only for your child, but for your own well-being.

■ *Judgment and society's reaction*

People sometimes attribute wrongful stigmas to noncustodial parents. One particular assumption is that noncustodial parents lost custody of the children because they were deemed to be unfit. This usually is not the case. Obviously, children of divorce cannot live with both parents at the same time, and so other arrangements must be made. Today many more parents are receiving shared custody so that both can have equal opportunities in the parenting responsibilities. Blended families experience equal custody more today than ever before.

Another common misconception is that parents are not able to participate in any social engagements when their children are with them. Lack of knowledge and understanding from others contribute to noncustodial parents' sense of isolation and make them feel like outcasts in normal society. Some of the feelings triggered by these misconceptions are hurt, anger, resentment, and loneliness, to name a few.

There are ways of dealing with these feelings. Single-parent groups can provide understanding and a sense of comradeship. Be assertive when you encounter a social prejudice. Talk with your friends about including you in their activities. The more active role you take in your life, the more you can deal with the pain and hurt of not having your children with you.

Custody Issues

More divorced parents share equally in the raising of their children today; this is known as *shared* (or *joint) custody.* There are several types of shared custody:

Shared legal custody: Each parent shares the legal responsibility for the child (i.e., medical, schooling, etc.).

Shared physical custody: The child lives with each of the parents for a portion of the time.

Shared legal and physical custody: Both parents have the legal and physical responsibilities for the children.

In shared custody a problem may arise when one parent does not fulfill his or her obligations. When children are living in more than one household, there must be a higher degree of communication and cooperation. Many divorced parents, due to the severity of the split in the family, have not developed the skill of communicating with one another after the divorce.

Sole custody indicates that one parent is responsible for the children, physically and legally. The other parent may have visitation rights but does not share the custody rights and duties. Many feel this is an outdated form of custody arrangement because it isolates one parent from the child. It is important that visitation rights be fair, and that noncustodial parents have ongoing input and choices in the raising of their children.

The belief is that the more input the parents have in the child's life, the more responsibility they will take in the care of the child. This sharing by both parents will promote a sense of continuity for the child in relation to both original parents.

Child support is another issue that can affect custody. The parents who do not pay support make it much more difficult for the parents who are trying to raise the children. There are several important principles to consider when dealing with this issue:

- Every child has the right to financial support and care from their respective parents.

- This payment of money should not be used as punishment. Often the parent paying child support uses payment as leverage when he or she is unhappy with visitation or other issues.

- Many parents, especially women, do not seek delinquent child-support payments, because they are concerned about their children's safety.

Children have the right to child support until they reach the age of emancipation, which is twenty-one. There are local and national groups that can help parents deal with the problems of child support. You should check with your local or state offices of Health and Human Services for child support legislation and enforcement in your area.

Common Problems

There are some common but severe problems that many blended families and ex-spouses have to deal with. They are complex situations and usually go on for an extended period of time, sometimes indefinitely. These problems are not found exclusively with the parents who are not living with their children; they also exist in the blended family itself. I'm referring to abandonment, addictions, mental illness, and physical or sexual abuse. Many times, these issues are the reason for the divorce. They persist and become part of the blended family because the offending parent may still have visitation rights with the children and may share custody.

How can families handle these problems? There are no easy answers, but there are some some important principles to remember:

- The partner whose ex-spouse has the problem should deal with the problem.

- Whatever the problem is, educate yourself on how to deal with the matter. For example, if your ex-spouse is an alcoholic, go to Al-Anon meetings for families of alcoholics and read some of the good books available on the subject.

- It is unwise and unfair to use children as pawns or spies in a legal battle concerning the former partners.

- Deal honestly with the children, educate them about the problem, and help them deal with the difficult circumstances. For instance, have them call you to come pick them up if their parent becomes intoxicated. Explain alcoholism to them, giving them books to read and helping them find support groups of their own.

- Safety first! If the children are not safe, take immediate action to protect them, and teach them to identify and report to you unsafe situations when they are on their visits.

- Seek mediation before going to court. First, talk to the parent involved to see if things can be worked out. If not, involve a mediator, third person, therapist, or court mediator before allowing it to become another traumatic legal battle.

- Seek court intervention if you or the child are in danger. The courts cannot work miracles and do not always rule in your favor. At times, the courts cannot protect individuals as much as they really need to be protected, especially in the case of battery. Even so, a parent should never hesitate to report child abuse or seek orders of protection if they become necessary.

FAMILY STORY TWO

Connie and Norm had two boys, ages ten and twelve. Their marriage broke up due to Norm's drinking, which he used to manage his manic-depressive disorder. When he was manic he would gamble, as well as disappear for days at a time; when depressed he would drink. He was careless with money and, therefore, very inconsistent with his child-support payments. There were times when he would behave inappropriately with the boys, yelling obscenities or leaving them alone in public places when angered. He would often not have enough money after gambling to feed the boys or to return them home to Connie. Connie had sole custody of the boys, but Norm had liberal visitation. Many times he would go for months without seeing the boys and then show up as though nothing had happened.

Connie married Sam in hope of giving the boys a more stable environment and a better role model. Sam's income was barely sufficient to meet the needs of a family of four. He believed strongly that the boys' father should help to support the boys. Shortly after Connie and Sam were married, Norm showed up. He was drunk and wanted to take the boys for a visit. The boys had not seen their father for a long time and showed reluctance to go with him. Norm became verbally abusive and physically attacked Sam when he tried to intercede. Connie had to call the police. ■

> How is it possible to co-parent with someone like Norm?
>
> Should it even be tried? If so, why?

The Goal: Co-Parenting

Co-parenting provides children with a sense of continuity throughout their growing-up years. On one level, it is detrimental for children to see the problems that a parent like Norm exhibits. On another level, though, it is better for them to see, and deal honestly with the truth about their backgrounds. Keeping secrets from children can be dangerous. They may later resent the lack of information about their families and feel that the problems were their fault.

■ *How to Co-Parent*

Face unresolved issues from the previous marriage. Connie needs to deal with Norm's alcoholism and manic-depressive disorder as the root of the problem. She must educate herself and her children and Sam on both of these disorders, and find support for the children.

Separate your roles as ex-spouse and as parent. Connie must realize that, although it is a burden, she has to be the responsible parent when Norm is not. Sam is there to be a support to her and the boys, but she is the one to deal with Norm because he is the boys' father. This is a tough order for anyone to fill, but it's necessary to the new family's survival.

Negotiate. Connie must arrange a time to talk to Norm when he is sober and not in a manic or severe depressive state. This in itself may be difficult. Due to the severity of the situation, she may have to enlist the services of a mediator if she cannot obtain Norm's cooperation. That would involve the services of an objective person. Norm would have to listen if he doesn't want to face court involvement. Connie needs to write out her expectations and clarify which ones she can be flexible about and which ones she must hold firm.

For example, a firm rule would be: no drinking, gambling, or foul language around the boys. Norm would pick them up, and return them, on a prescheduled basis. He would pay regular child support or his wages would be garnished. Enrollment in an alcoholism treatment program would be mandatory, as well as receiving medication for his manic-depression. Connie could go with him to the first appointment, to make sure an accurate picture was given. Otherwise, she could get a restraining order, due to his behavior at the house. If he showed up at the house again in that condition, she could call the police immediately and not allow him to see the boys. She could also ask him about his needs and his stipulations concerning his visitation times with the boys.

Develop an ongoing system. Set up a schedule of visitation that both partners agree on. Set up guidelines for dealing with the children. Allow a reasonable amount of time to put these systems into effect before trying something else.

Involve the children. After you and your ex-spouse have negotiated some of the more difficult situations, involve the children, asking for their ideas. Let them express their wishes and fears to both parents. Ask them what guidelines they think are fair for both households.

Connie and Norm's boys were able to tell their father, in front of an alcoholism counselor, how frightened and angry they were. They stated that they did not want to see him when he was drunk or abusive, but they made it clear that they wanted him in their lives.

Focus on the needs of the children. The children are not pawns in this game to use against each other. Realize the importance of coming together, as parents, to try to establish what is best for them. Children need to have access to both parents in a healthy environment. The healthier parent should keep reinforcing this, but in a way that encourages both adults to focus on what is best for the children. Sometimes even parents who are ill will be more reasonable for the good of their children.

Choose what to control and how. This is a big issue, especially for the parent who bears the burden of dealing with problems. The temptation is to try to totally control the problem, but it is more realistic for those in charge to pick their issues carefully and not be driven crazy trying to manage every detail. The main problem lies with the troubled parent who holds the entire blended family under emotional siege. Each member has to learn how to cope, so that he or she isn't victimized by the other parent in their family. The family should work through their feelings and develop some problem-solving techniques.

Connie and Sam had talks on their own about dealing with Norm's problems. Then they talked to the boys and gave them an opportunity to express their feelings about their father. In this way, Connie and Sam were exercising control over their immediate family. They could not totally control Norm's behavior, but they could deal with his behavior by taking charge of their own lives.

Aim for mutual solutions. Both parents should try to agree on some solutions to the problems they are having. This is difficult, especially if the other parent will not admit his or her problems. Cite what is good for the children and set some firm limits. Emphasize that you want to settle this without going to court but that you will pursue legal means if necessary. The parent who is in denial must be made to work with you on some realistic solutions. The key here is to be realistic. Connie did not expect Norm's behavior to change overnight, but she did expect him to get into treatment and not drink around the boys.

Be consistent with your word. The negotiating will not work if the other parent knows you are bluffing or will cave in under pressure. Neither will it work if you are judgmental, self-righteous, or condemning. You must be consistent and firm, yet open to hearing and empathizing with the other parent.

Safety first. It can't be emphasized too much that if there is any question of danger or child abuse, the protection of the court and police should be sought. At no time should such behavior be tolerated.

Dealing with a parent who has severe problems is an added burden on the new blended family. Take past and present problems into account before bringing the new family together. It requires much patience and work to deal with a troubled parent in the family.

Other Problems

There are some other problems with ex-spouses that are common but not as severe. The ex-spouse may maintain a lifestyle you are opposed to. Or he or she may be too passive, not participating as actively in parenting as you feel is necessary. The previously listed principles can apply to these kinds of situations as well, but can be implemented in a less stringent way.

Talking about feelings and getting outside support are two of the ways in which many people deal with difficult members of their blended families. Embracing more realistic expectations and goals that include ex-spouses can enable the entire family to move into a new place of acceptance and love.

8
A New Family Order
Establishing and Enjoying a New Family

Marion and Ron, married for over a year, lived in a new house with their four children from previous marriages. Marion had three children: Mary, age ten; Doug, age eight; and Amy, age six. Ron had a fourteen-year-old son, Marty, and a twenty-three-year-old son who lived on his own.

Marion and Ron very much wanted to have a child of their own as soon as the family was ready. They believed it was important to teach the children certain values that would make the household a pleasant place. But they also realized that, coming from such diverse backgrounds, it would be difficult to establish a common ground for everyone in the family.

Marion's ex-husband took the children to his house, with his wife and child, every other weekend. Ron's son went to spend the summer with his mother in another state. Marion and Ron were left trying to coordinate the guidelines and values of three households! Each member of the household, including the co-parents, had his or her unique needs—each of which would have to be considered when setting up the new family.

They set up a series of meetings with different family members to gain insight into each person's needs. Marion first met with her three children to hear what was important to them. All three wanted reassurance that the new family would be a stable and lasting one. They also said they needed to have their own, individual space within the household. They posed questions

133

about Ron's methods of discipline, his anger threshold, and the types of punishment they might expect from him. They wondered if the rules in their new home would apply when they visited their father on weekends.

Marion reassured them that the whole family would meet during the next week in order to discuss all those issues. She made it clear that the new family must be helpful for each member, and any rules would be used for that purpose. She promised to meet with their father to try to set up some joint guidelines but explained that there would be differences in the two families that everyone would have to get used to.

The children seemed relieved to be involved in the decisions of their new family and went off to their rooms to write down their ideas.

Ron had the same talk with his son, Marty. He asked him what he thought he needed from the family, what rules he thought were appropriate for his age, and what he wanted his relationship with Marion to be like. At first, Marty was hesitant to talk, saying that he didn't know what he wanted. Ron encouraged him by saying how important Marty's input was and that he didn't want Marty to feel left out of the family because he was older. Ron said that he realized it would be inappropriate for Marty to have the same rules as the younger children. Marty brightened at that and began to share some of his thoughts: he didn't want to be treated like a baby; he longed for time alone with Ron; and he wanted his mother to be part of all major decisions. He was unsure of what role he wanted Marion to play in his life. He liked her, but he wasn't sure how much he wanted her telling him what to do. He was ambivalent about his relationship with his new sisters and brother. He wanted to get to know them, but he wasn't sure how close he wanted to be to them. They got on his nerves sometimes, and he was jealous when Ron spent time with them. He also expressed the need for a space of his own in the house. He said sometimes he liked the family activities and other times he didn't. He also said he didn't know where his mother fit into all these plans, and he did not want to leave her behind.

Ron listened intently and praised Marty for sharing his feelings so forthrightly and honestly. He was just as honest in saying that he didn't have the answers to all these questions, but he agreed to work on them with Marty and help him feel secure within the new family. He voiced his love for Marty, saying that he respected Marty's need to explore and develop his relationship with Marion and the other children in his own way. He understood and sympathized with Marty's feelings about his mother and said he would support that bond. Marty was visibly relieved and agreed to attend the family meeting the following week. ■

How did Ron and Marion set the stage for their new family?

What problems do you think they have already avoided by having these discussions with their children?

In this chapter, we will talk about how to define your new family, how to set up family guidelines, and how to seek outside resources in the development of the blended family.

Defining Your Family

We have talked in previous chapters about knowing who the members of your family are. This is especially true in the co-parenting situation. New boundaries must be set up within the family that allow every child to move as easily as possible between households. Generally, blended families have an increased number of people living under one roof.

Setting up new guidelines and boundaries for each member of the new household helps everyone feel like they belong. As we will discover, this is *only* true if each member of the family has input in setting up the guidelines. Marion and Ron were careful to ask all the children for their input. Within the structure of a family meeting, every individual was allowed equal say in contributing ideas.

■ *Openness*

We can't stress enough the importance of honesty. Openness, in setting up the new family, is crucial in three ways:

Every member of the family needs the appropriate amount of information if they are to handle their feelings and commit to the new family. That is to say, children need to know what their new parents have been through and are thinking, and parents need to know what their children are feeling.

Openness also has to do with acceptance. Other people in the family, whether children or co-parents, must feel accepted for their differences. This requires flexibility on the part of each person.

Openness encourages each member to talk about feelings without fear of judgment. It also sets a precedent for verbalizing, rather than acting out, those feelings.

The Family Setup: Meeting the Needs of Its Members

It is important to ask, "What is the purpose of a family?" What are family members meant to do for each other? Parents get married because of their love for one another, but doesn't the family go beyond that?

Each of us needs to belong, to be loved, to be safe. Children need food, shelter, and a place in which to learn how to grow and develop into mature adults. Meeting the needs of the other members of the family, as well as your own, should be the goal of setting up the new family. If parents can operate on that principle, they will be much less likely to be punitive or authoritarian toward the children. Each person's action can be seen as expressing a need that the family could help to fulfill. Ron and Marion understood that principle when they explored their children's needs before establishing the family guidelines.

■ Giving back and forth: mutuality

As the blended family lives together, its members gradually come to see the overall goal of meeting one another's needs. But from the beginning, the parents must have this goal clearly before them; they are responsible for meeting their children's needs.

Children learn by example; they learn that giving and meeting the needs of others bring personal satisfaction. They experience receiving from their parents and wish to emulate compassion in their own lives.

■ *Patterns of behavior that indicate unmet needs*

How can parents know and meet the needs of every person in the family? Examining Marion and Ron's family story may help blended families uncover some of their hidden needs.

The children in the family story voiced several needs. They needed to be in touch with both biological parents. They needed information about behaviors and discipline within their new home. They needed space of their own, and they needed to be heard. We will discuss these issues later in this chapter. In a successful situation, the following usually happens:

- A person's needs become obvious—something is troubling him or her.

- The person will act out those needs in some way, either through distressing behavior, verbalization, or withdrawal.

- Someone within the family attempts to meet the other family member's needs.

- Peace, in some form, is restored to the household.

———————— FAMILY STORY ————————

One afternoon, shortly after Ron and Marty's talk about the family meeting, Marty came home from school in a bad mood. He slammed the back door, threw his books on the floor, growled at his sisters who were sitting in the kitchen, and locked himself in his room. Ron was not home from work yet, and Marion wondered how to handle the situation. She remembered that Marty had been having a difficult time adjusting to his new school, and she thought that might be part of the problem.

With his books in her hand, Marion knocked on Marty's bedroom door and asked if he was all right. He told her to leave him alone. When Marion said she would leave his books by the door, there was no response. When asked if she could get him anything, Marty answered with a resounding, "NO!" Marion said that she would like to help him but didn't want to push him if he wasn't ready. She let him know she would check back with him after a while and that she would be in the kitchen if he needed her.

Marion's girls seemed a bit frightened and silent as music from Marty's room blared throughout the house. Marion explained to them that she thought Marty was having a hard time going to a new school and that he might need some kind words. One of the girls suggested that they make some cookies for him. They had just finished putting the first batch in the oven when the music coming from Marty's room subsided. He came slowly out of his room, looking glum. One of the girls said they were making some cookies to help him feel better. He looked a bit startled and mumbled thanks under his breath. Marion suggested that the girls play games downstairs while she and Marty finished in the kitchen. After the girls left, Marty sat down at the kitchen table with his head down, not looking at Marion.

She asked him how things had gone at school that day. He did not answer at first. Then he asked, rather accusingly, "Why did you and my father take me out of my other school?" Marion paused to consider the best answer to give, considering his mood. She said that when the family moved to the new house he had to go to a new school. Marty responded with a snort and said, "That's not fair!" Marion agreed that it wasn't as fair to him as to the other children. She said she was sorry about what he was going through. Marty looked surprised but then responded with, "I'll bet!" Marion gave him some cookies and asked what she could do for him, and he responded by saying that he wanted to go back to his old school. She reflected that he must miss his friends there. He said he did and admitted that he feared he wouldn't be able to keep up his grades. At this point, he was close to tears.

Marion offered to help Marty with his homework, saying that she used to be a tutor when she was on her own with the girls. He showed some surprise, saying that he hadn't known that before and then apologized for being such a brat. She told him there was no way he could be a brat, at which point he grinned and reached for another cookie. ■

What did Marion focus on rather than Marty's behavior?

How did this situation ultimately help them to know one another better?

This volatile situation was defused when Marion looked through what was happening and saw signals for help in her stepson. She picked up on Marty's needs and his accompanying fears that the needs would not be met. If Marion had merely punished him, she would have alienated him and made his pain and sense of not belonging even worse. Then he would have acted out his needs even further.

■ *Survival*

Survival is a primary goal of the blended family. Members of new families like Marion's have already seen several families broken apart due to some type of dysfunction. We do not need to contribute to further dysfunction by insisting on one person's authority, sensitivities, and rules. Marion put the survival of the family above Marty's ability to hurt her feelings. Disrespect is not acceptable, but sometimes there is a higher goal to be considered, and you have to "choose your battles," so to speak.

On the other hand, if someone in the family is badly damaged and is, therefore, determined to destroy the family, action must be taken. *No one member, including a parent, should be allowed to dominate or destroy the family.*

Relationships

Chapter 4 discussed bonding as the way to establish relationships in the family. If your family is organized around meeting the needs of its members, you will have a bonded family. It is through the relationships in the family that individuals, especially children, learn to develop into independent, functioning adults. *The relationships within the family should be the basis for the guidelines and consequences that are agreed upon.*

The focus in any family should not be the children's good behavior, but the relationships that develop with each member of the family, including the co-parents and the extended family. When Marty apologized for his behavior, he was recognizing his disrespect to Marion and was responding in kind to her respect for him. This is a better lesson than any negative punishment could instill. They were moving toward a relationship that no amount of correction or discipline could have brought about.

As we discuss setting up a new family order, we will use the word *guideline* rather than *rule,* because *rule* often has a negative and authoritative meaning. The purpose of setting up guidelines in your family is twofold:

1. To meet the needs of the people in the family

2. To provide balance and order in the family, which enables its members to exhibit self-control

■ Discipleship—not punishment

The concept of discipleship, rather than punishment, actually comes from the example of Christ and his disciples. Did Christ punish his disciples in order to gain their allegiance? On the contrary, he had such love for them and showed such an example throughout his life that they wanted to be like him. He illustrated the highest form of empathy by giving up his own life to ease the spiritual suffering of humankind. Parents need to follow that example, as Marion did when she empathized with Marty's difficulties in school. Her patient way of handling the situation taught Marty the value of self-control and respect for others.

When a person respects himself he treats others with respect. In the case of blended families, there is the added shame and self-doubt due to the breakup of the original families. Consequently, there is not an abundance of self-respect. Parents cannot teach their children self-respect unless they practice it themselves. So steps must be taken that will heal the feelings of shame and inadequacy left by previous family problems. As you model respect for yourself and for others, your children will learn self-respect, and thus, respect for others.

We show one another respect through empathy: putting ourselves in the other person's shoes and feeling what that person is feeling. When we try to understand what our chil-

dren are going through and show them that we understand
and care, we are respecting them. Children can respond obe-
diently in this kind of atmosphere, whereas obedience out of
fear of being punished destroys the relationship.

The aggression that is so pervasive in this world should not
be perpetuated within the family. This happens when children
are treated in a punitive manner, and that aggression is carried
into their adulthood. It is only through love and respect that
children learn to exercise self-control.

■ *Ways of setting up guidelines*

What does a family do when one individual is disrespectful or
won't play his or her part? Is there some system that can be
implemented to help things run more smoothly? Yes, there
are some guidelines, but no one system will work all the time
or with every family. The key is setting up an individual
family system that works for you. Perhaps the key term should
be *problem solving.* If you see the conflicts in your family as a
group problem to solve, instead of merely unacceptable behavior
that you as the parent have to get rid of, you will be much more
successful. I often say to the kids I work with: "I wonder what
we can do about solving this?" This tells them that I am not
threatening them for their behavior. Rather, I am willing to work
with them on what is bothering them.

Setting up guidelines requires a great deal of problem solving and trial and error. The following is a format for setting
up some family guidelines.

Discussion. As was seen in the family story, Marion and
Ron set up discussions with their children. At first they
met separately to gauge the children's individual needs,
and then they came together to set up guidelines the whole
family could live with.

143

Each child in Marion and Ron's family identified a need for privacy and space. It was then up to the entire family to decide on guidelines that would respect that need. Blended families have lived through many rules in previous settings, some of which have been tremendously damaging. In the new household, every family member should be involved in the discussion process. Listening should be the major task of these sessions. Children often do not share their feelings because they have not been listened to or taken seriously. In the discussion process, children must have equal input in identifying problems and saying what they think the guidelines should be. They might not always have the final say, but if they are listened to and given a chance to give their opinion they will feel respected. Then they can better live with the family's final decision because the relationship remains intact.

During discussions, pick one subject at a time—don't try to solve all the family problems in one sitting. Too large an agenda can overwhelm everyone, and then the fighting starts. If the discussion gets too heated, table the family meeting until the next day. Parents must help children to refocus and keep the meeting on track with love, understanding, and empathy. It may help to have a discussion about the guidelines for the actual meetings, so that each family member is guaranteed a chance to be heard without criticism. You will be surprised how many ideas your children will come up with if you will ask their opinion.

Election. Whenever possible, family guidelines should be decided and established by the family as a group. Marion and Ron set up a family meeting the next week to establish guidelines and goals with the entire family involved. One person in the family cannot possibly make all the rules or understand the needs of every other member of the household. If the person making all the rules is the stepparent, as in the family story of chapter 6, problems arise because bonding has not yet taken place. People are much more likely to obey guidelines if they have helped to set them up.

Consider how your conscience has developed. When someone just told you what to do before you understood the right or wrong of it, your obedience—if that was your response—was not really your choice. Many times this may have caused resentment and did not teach you to make responsible choices on your own. However, as children take part in setting up guidelines, they develop their own internal sense of right and wrong and learn how to make informed choices.

I have seen families sit down every week and draw up a chart as to what chores each person will do. Each person has some choice in the matter. Some families take a vote on particular issues, with parents having the right to modify the results. Children already have a sense that their parents should have more responsibility—and therefore more say in a matter. But it is important to them to add their input and to be taken seriously.

Consequences. The word *consequences* will be used here in place of *punishment* because the latter term often means physical or emotional aggression from someone in an authoritative position. *Punishment may bring about obedience, but it does not instill the sense of internal self-control that should carry a child into adulthood. It also destroys the relationship and love for the parent that has not yet fully developed in the blended family.*

However, limits and boundaries in family life must be set up. I like the word *consequences* because it helps children to see the natural order of events and the way our actions affect the world around us. For example, parent and child may agree that the child can buy a toy out of her allowance and that, therefore, she cannot spend all her allowance on candy. If she does spend it on candy, she will have no money for the toy and won't be able to buy it. This is not a punishment; it is the natural result of her spending all her money. If it is agreed that the child will take a nap before going to the slumber party, but the afternoon has been filled with tantrums and fighting with brothers and sisters because she didn't take a nap and became grumpy, the natural consequence is that she doesn't get to go to the slumber party.

It is important that the consequence match the behavior as closely as possible. I have seen examples of children spending six hours in their room because they did not eat their peas at lunch, when they never liked peas to begin with. By the same token, some children talk to parents in rude and unacceptable ways and the parents ignore the behavior. Neither end of the spectrum—punitive or permissive behavior—is healthy for the child or the family.

Families need to discuss consequences and come up with some standard ones that all members can agree on. Some families set up consequences that are written and posted for all to see, and these apply to all members of the family. Other situations—and there will always be unexpected situations—will have to be handled as they come up.

It's a good idea to sit down with the child at the time of the problem and ask, "What do you think we should do about this, and what should the consequences be?" Children often judge their own actions much more harshly than their parents would; in this kind of situation you are put in the position of granting mercy (by giving a "lighter sentence"), rather than enforcing your own rule.

The entire process of discussing, electing, and choosing consequences is one of *developing alternatives*. Regular family meetings keep the system working and teach children how to make informed and mature choices, free of punishment and blame.

Praise must be given regularly to all members of the blended family, regardless of the difficulties they had that day. Families sometimes become so focused on guidelines and consequences that they forget the basic task of making one another feel loved and appreciated. The tendency is to give praise as a reward for good behavior, instead of allowing it to be an expression of appreciation for the person. An "I'm glad you're here today" can go a long way in soothing a troubled child. Many parents who come into my office say that they cannot think of one positive attribute to praise their child for; much of the time these parents were never praised themselves when they were children. These painful family patterns must be broken if the family is to come together.

■ *Difficult behavior*

What can parents do in the face of lying, stealing, open defiance, or an impasse? What happens when there isn't agreement in the family?

In an impasse situation, where there is no agreement at any stage, you may need to postpone the discussion or family meeting until tempers have cooled. If it is a situation where someone in the family is being hurt, it may be necessary to take action while displaying as much respect as possible for all the parties concerned.

"I'm sorry you are so upset about something that you keep hitting your younger brother. Until we figure out what is bothering you, you will have to be separated from him except with supervision. I'm sorry about this, but all members of the family must be safe."

Separation or "time out" can be a good way of calming down unresolved situations. Family members need one another and do not like being excluded. Separation must never be lengthy or threatened to be permanent.

In the case of a child's open defiance, the parent must realize that this is an issue of respect. Somehow the child has lost respect or is angry about something that has happened. To begin with, the child probably has not had enough time to develop respect for the stepparent *as a parent*. Therefore, the parents involved should talk to the child in a very empathetic manner about times in his life when he did not feel respected. In this way, the child is encouraged to share hurt feelings instead of lashing out.

Adults can easily forget what it was like to be children and in that forgetfulness offend their children's sensibilities. We do this by talking "over" them, for example, or talking about them in front of others, or ignoring their feelings. Children learn much more by how we treat them than by what we tell them. A classic example of this is parents who yell at each other in front of the children or berate the children because of their own frustrations. Then when the children yell at *them,* they are severely punished or the parent is devastated. The parents can't figure out why their children would treat them like this, but the children are merely doing what they have seen the parents do, and they are angry at the treatment they have seen and received.

The same principles apply to lying and stealing. Lying and stealing are signs that the child is acting out a deeper hurt. The parents must find the cause by listening and interpreting. When children lie, it is because they believe they will not be listened to. They either say what they think their parents want to hear, or they lie in order to avoid punishment. Lying is sometimes an indication that punishment has been too severe or that the child believes his behavior is more important than he is. There are two ways of dealing with lying:

1. Tell the child that something must be very wrong or he would be telling the truth.

2. Ask him how he thinks it makes the family feel when he lies. This can only be done if you have a relationship with the child and after some interpretation has been done. I tell children that there is no such thing as a lie in my office, because everything they say and do means something. Our job is to find out what they mean by what they are saying! I almost always get the same reaction: they are delighted that they are being understood. There is much less lying from that point on.

When a child steals, he tells us that there is a need of his that is not being fulfilled. Children at the children's home steal from each other all the time because they are deprived of their parents' presence and love. They try to fill themselves up with possessions to make up for the emptiness inside. We talk about what they need most, acknowledge the grief they feel, and try to substitute a stuffed animal, a blanket, and more staff attention. Children often steal when they are young because they do not distinguish other people's possessions from their own. If they live in the house, everything must be theirs. They must be taught to develop empathy for others. Ask them: "How do you think it makes your sister feel when you take her hair ribbon? How would it make you feel if she took yours?"

Older children may be feeling angry and looking for a way to express it. Taking them to the store they stole from and letting them confront the store manager and seeing your and their embarrassment is a good way of assisting them in internalizing a deeper sense of right and wrong.

If a child's behavior in these areas becomes unmanageable and threatening to the family, then it is time to seek professional help from a qualified therapist to uncover the roots of the behavior and give the child added comfort, instead of continuing his and the family's suffering. More will be written about this at the end of the chapter.

Co-Parenting Coordination

Now that you are just beginning to get a system down in your own family, how do you carry over some of these guidelines in the co-parenting relationship when your children may be members of more than one household? It is not uncommon to hear such refrains as: "Daddy doesn't make me do chores when I'm at his house!" Just as you have discussions at your house, you must have a discussion time with your co-parent to help set up some guidelines that will apply to both households. Some suggested topics are: bedtimes, issues of self-respect, lying, stealing, chores, consequences, and school. The more continuity the better, especially for younger children.

If you can agree on the larger principles of self-respect—openness and no unjust punishments—you have come a long way. Your goal is to do what is best for the children; the guidelines should not turn into a power struggle between the co-parents.

Talk to the children together if possible but at least separately. Explain that the guidelines will be different because you are two different people and that you all have to try extra hard to cooperate. Tell them you are sorry they have had to go through the divorce and that you realize children should not have to be put through this. But this is the family they have now, and you will try to support them the best way you can. As to "Daddy doesn't make me," you can respond with, "I know you miss your father, and I'm sorry, but when you're at this house you have to go by the guidelines we've all agreed upon." This is the advantage of discussion; you can remind them that *they* agreed on these guidelines.

When Should You Seek Outside Help?

If a family has repeatedly tried and failed to come up with a system that works for them, then it may be time to look for some outside help from a therapist. In this country, especially in religious circles, there is still an unfortunate stigma about therapy. The facts are that no family can meet everyone's needs. Blended families have more than their share of pressures and pain. Just as premarital counseling helps many couples prepare for a new union, so might therapy prove helpful to blended families. It is simply too much for most families to deal with all the losses and pain represented by their members. In the case of more serious problems, such as an alcoholic or emotionally ill ex-spouse, or children with hyperactivity or learning disabilities, outside help is definitely a must.

When many parents first come to see me they express a common feeling: They feel they have run out of resources to solve what is happening in the family. They feel their family, and possibly a particular member, is out of control. Many times they do not feel able to handle the situation in a positive manner. They are angry at a particular child for his or her behavior. *When there is someone in your family expressing a behavior that is disruptive or out of control and it is met by you or other members of the family with a similar out-of-con-*

trol response, it is time for outside help. Many times, one member of the family is merely expressing the pain of the rest of the family. The family is so upset that they can no longer see the problems clearly. Sometimes a therapist can help you deal with these buried problems.

■ *Choosing a therapist*

The specific needs of your family will determine the kind of therapist you seek. There are steps you can take to find the best help and therefore move your family forward.

Get a good referral, either from a pastor, a doctor, a friend who has been in therapy, or from their therapist. If possible, the person referring should know you, so he or she can match up your family's personality with that of the therapist.

The couple should have an initial session with the therapist, to see if they feel comfortable.

Write down questions to ask the therapist, and see if you are comfortable with the answers. Do not go to someone if you don't feel comfortable with him or her. If you have questions about the therapist's belief system or the type of therapy he or she uses, ask for further information. Do not assume that because the therapist has the same spiritual beliefs as you he is qualified to treat your family; he must have expertise in the area of your problem, i.e., depression, child therapy, etc.

■ *What should a therapist do?*

A therapist should not do the work for the family! The answers are inside you and your family; the therapist merely helps you to see them. Beware of therapists who are quick to provide easy answers or tell you what to do. They need to listen carefully to get a full picture and let you do most of the talking, especially in the beginning.

A good therapist will help each person identify and develop skills to meet his or her own needs. Once the dust has settled and each person feels heard, the therapist can help you come up with insights, ideas, and problem-solving techniques that are right for your family.

The therapist should be willing to provide additional resources if needed. If there are outside problems, such as alcoholism, that need ongoing support groups, it is the therapist's responsibility to put the family or individual members in contact with competent help. Some of these resources will be with you long after you leave the therapist's office.

In the case of mental illness or criminal behavior, a therapist should help with alternative arrangements such as hospitalization for the person who cannot function within the family. This of course is only in the most severe case, after other options have been exhausted.

In developing a new family order, time and patience are of the essence. This will not happen overnight, and each family member needs time to find his or her own place in the family. If members of the family can see that the goal in building a family is for every person in it to find a comfortable place in which to grow, they will develop the empathy and love that we all need and want from our families.

9
Spiritual Journeys
*How Blended Families Can Forgive
and Come Together*

Martha had become increasingly discouraged over the course of the last year. She envisioned her home being a loving environment in which to raise her daughter and her husband's two boys, but instead, the bedlam grew progressively worse. The noise of it had driven her to seek some answers from someone outside the family. Her husband, Steve, tried to reassure her that the problems they were having in their year-old marriage were due to having normal teenagers under one roof. His boys were thirteen and fifteen, and Martha's daughter was twelve going on thirty.

Martha had a friend, Joyce, who was a stepmother to three children. Martha had always admired Joyce because she was able to talk about her own feelings, as well as respect the feelings of her family. Joyce told Martha that the family had worked through some pretty tough problems and that in the five years they had been living together, only the last few years had been rewarding.

Joyce mentioned that she belonged to a women's support group, which gave her strength through journal writing and developing life goals. Martha thought the group sounded strange, and she wondered how writing events down could give a person support. She had enough demands on her time, without the added burden of keeping a journal.

Nevertheless, Martha called Joyce one morning, seeking a friend to talk and cry with. She felt that Joyce had another dimension to her life that she might need to examine. She knew that Joyce believed in God. Martha grew up in a very religious home, but she could not get past that point. Steve believed that religious beliefs were private and didn't feel comfortable talking about such matters. The family said grace at meals and went to church, but they did not talk about their own beliefs. Steve and Martha wanted to teach their children something about God but did not know where to begin when the family was in such turmoil. ■

Does Steve and Martha's dilemma sound familiar?

How does a family that has experienced a significant amount of pain and whose members come from different backgrounds find their way to a faith that will aid them in bringing their family together?

Why is there even a need for spiritual input in the family?

Your Spiritual Journey

The purpose of a spiritual journey is to help you come closer to yourself, God, and your family. There are two major questions that must be asked when talking or writing about this journey:

1. How do I define a spiritual journey?

2. How do I start, and where do I start?

Maybe we should talk about the second one first. You start on your journey right where you are. A spiritual journey might be defined as an individual's personal search for a close relationship with God.

I want to address my comments in this chapter to all people of faith or who are seeking a faith. I realize that many of the people reading this book are from the Christian faith. Maybe you do have an established faith, but you feel your faith has let you down in this new family situation. My goal for this chapter is to help all of us develop some skills that can add another dimension to our faith, one that will enable us to bring our families together through forgiveness and restoration.

I do not think that forgiveness can be complete unless we have some help from the outside—the kind of spiritual help that will cleanse our souls and help us feel loved and forgiven ourselves. This divine power will fuel our empathy to forgive in situations that would otherwise be impossible.

Maybe faith or a belief system has not been a part of your life before, or you're not even sure of your feelings about God, but you want to investigate for yourself.

How to begin

Realize that God is where you are. Many times blended families feel shame from their church's teachings. They equate the church's opinion with God's opinion. If they have felt rejection and judgment, then they think God is displeased with them. If there is unresolved conflict in the family, then God must not be blessing them or helping them.

Those are all myths that are taught in childhood, but many people continue to be haunted by them. Scripture states that God is love. Christ knocks at the door of our lives, always willing to enter if we will only give entry.

In my own spiritual journey, it has taken me many years to separate present beliefs from legalism. My own prayer, journal writing, and meditation have helped me to exchange those old messages for new ones of love and acceptance. However, each individual has to make her own journey and begin her search.

Our journey begins with a search to open ourselves to God. Martha began her spiritual journey by asking Joyce questions about her support group and her journal writing. She sought out a friend of similar background with whom she could feel safe. We must realize that our journey starts with small steps. We must allow ourselves to move toward God in a way that feels safe and yet challenging to us.

God accepts us just as we are, where we are. We will explore this aspect of God later when we talk about forgiveness. Christ promises all who come to him will never be turned away (John 6:37).

Open yourself up to God. Through prayer and meditation we can connect with a personal God. We must start here by being willing—or recognizing our need—to know God better, to come closer and seek divine help. We need help for our family that is struggling to be born. The birth depends on each person's own spiritual birth to give us more forgiveness, empathy, and love.

If you are like many people, it may be difficult to pray, or prayer might not yet be in your experience. Again, start where you are, either by telling God your concerns, reading something you find helpful, or talking to someone you are comfortable with on the subject.

While in a spiritual direction program (a program designed to help people come closer to God), I went on an afternoon retreat with my spiritual director.

We had written down various topics for prayer, but I kept coming back to the question of how one discovers the "real" God of love and mercy, as opposed to the judgmental God our religious culture has often set before us. We spent over an hour sitting in a lovely chapel, talking conversationally with God, as we would with another person. After a time, my spiritual director left me alone in the chapel, encouraging me to find my own ways of getting closer to God. I sat for a long time, praying, and was suddenly confronted by a personal revelation, as the phrase, "I give you my soul" swept through my mind.

I had been to church all my life, had an early "conversion" experience, and had been to study with Francis Schaeffer at L'Abri Fellowship, where I had a genuine faith experience. This, however, was another level for me, opening myself to God and saying, "I want to know your presence in my life."

I am sharing my experiences to illustrate that we are all fellow travelers on this journey, and *even if we have had a genuine spiritual life for some time,* there is always more to learn and new aspects of God to experience. We are not in a race or a competition to become the "most spiritual" person; we are seeking the help of God in meeting our own and our family's needs.

■ *How to begin a journal*

In several chapters I've stressed the importance of journal writing, but here we will explore the process more fully in the context of deepening our relationship with God. Luci Shaw, a poet and noted journal writer, wrote an enlightening book on journal writing called *Life Path*. She states that a journal need not be set up into two parts, one secular and one spiritual, because all of life is a spiritual search, whether we are at church, or doing the dishes, or fighting with one of our children. We need a way to let out our emotions from all of these activities and to find God in them. A journal can also be a place to express our requests and prayers. We need a private place, a place where we can say whatever we feel and ask whatever questions come to mind. In this way we find where we are in our spiritual journey.

There is no one correct way to journal, but there have been some good books written on the subject, which I have listed in the bibliography section. The key is finding a routine that helps you to write down your feelings and express the events of the day, your questions and prayers. You can design your journal in whatever ways are helpful to you.

Getting started might be the most difficult task.

Set aside a time and place to write where you will not be disturbed, even if it's only for fifteen minutes, twice a day. People often complain that they don't have time to keep a journal, but, as one meditation book stated, we need to take the time. Focusing on what is important, and gaining guidance through prayer, focuses our mind and organizes the day.

It is easier to get things done when we take time to relax and organize our thoughts and feelings. Journals do not have to be organized in order to bring ideas and personal perspectives closer to the surface and provide valuable insights into family life.

I had a client who had four children, all of whom were young and very active. She wondered how she could ever find time alone until we came up with the idea of including the children in the journal writing process. This was a special time, where the children could write in their own journals or draw pictures of their day, while Mom did hers in her room, too. After twenty minutes, they came back to their mother for a cuddle and the chance to share their journal or picture of their choice. Then everyone had treats! What a wonderful way to teach your children that their thoughts, feelings, and prayers are important. If this didn't work every day, it wasn't the end of the world. She also enlisted the help of her husband with the children at night. After they were in bed, she could journal some more if needed.

I have known people, myself included, who journal on trains, in restaurants, on a park bench, or at the beach. Journal writing can take place just about anywhere that one can put pen to paper. I carry my journal with me so that I can write during my breaks, or when something occurs to me that I feel I must write down.

I especially like to write down my dreams, so I keep my journal on my bedside table at night so I can write them down before I forget them in the morning. I believe that God speaks to us through our dreams, and that they are important symbols of our emotional lives. (John Sanford explores these ideas further in his book, *Dreams and Healing*. See the recommended readings on page 199.)

Start where you are. Many people start by writing whatever comes to their mind each day, whatever they are feeling— their struggles, joys, trips, questions, events, prayers, and thoughts. Some people include meaningful passages of Scripture or statements from others. Some days you may write only a few sentences; other days you may have pages. The goal is to write every day, but that doesn't always happen. Journal writing isn't something that should cause you stress or anxiety. A journal can become a kind of friend that provides emotional and spiritual release. In time, it can bring focus and clarity to your life and family and become part of the natural order of things.

For those people who are having difficulty starting a journal, it might be easier to begin by addressing one specific question. Example: What am I feeling right now? What event has most moved me today or this week, and why?

When I first started working with my spiritual director, he asked me to write an autobiography about my spiritual life. As I wrote of the events and people who had been significant in my life, I was surprised to see the progression of God's work at every stage, including my most rebellious. Pick one event or person in your life that has affected you and why, if you need a topic to start.

Remember, a journal is one's own, and it is for every individual to decide if it will be a shared or private thing. When I ask my clients to keep a journal, they are never required to share their writing with me.

Explore your pain. Did you notice how Martha admired Joyce for how she handled the situations with her family? It was not because Joyce had a perfect family or handled her conflicts in such a way, but because she had a friend, her journal. She would write down everything that happened each day, including her rage, her hurt, her joy, her wonderment, her confusion. Whatever her experience, she had an outlet. She could go back later and look at her entries to see what had happened in her family. She could also write out something she thought might help her get through another day. Journal writing is a cathartic process, which needn't be edited or revised to meet others' expectations.

In a blended family it is difficult to sort out all the emotions. Keeping a journal is one way of doing that, and when you are having a bad day you can look back in your journal and see what the last bad day looked like and how you handled it.

Some people are still afraid of their pain. One woman said to me, "Oh, I could never stand to see everything written in front of me like that!" My response was, "Then write down only what you can take, and leave the rest for when you are ready." The fear is often worse than the remembrance, so take it a day at a time.

Bridge the gap to prayer and meditation. It is not easy to waltz into the presence of God. God is always available, but it is difficult to perceive a Being that can't be seen or touched. We need something to help us on our way; a journal comes alive through the written word. The apostle Paul, in his letter to the Roman church, states that the Spirit of God is well aware of our weakness and prays for us with "sighs too deep for words" (Romans 8:26). The journal puts words to our sighs and to the sighs of the members of our new family.

A journal can also help express spiritual questions. We cannot gain strength from God until we are willing to be honest with our questions. Throughout Scripture, there is evidence of God's patient and understanding nature. God stood with every mistake, forgave and helped each person— king, prophet, peasant, and disciple—to deal with the results of their actions, and never stopped loving them. I think God desires and understands our questions. One principle Francis Schaeffer taught me is that we may not always be able to understand the answers, but no question is too hard, or unacceptable to, God.

Luci Shaw and others have suggested writing letters to God. A letter helps us to see what questions we have and gives us the ability to get closer to God with those questions. The journal is a way of talking to God in a natural, comfortable way.

Journal writing has helped me to read the Bible and other spiritual materials, giving me a place to write down prayers that are meaningful to me. My journal is a private communication between God and myself, which no one judges or measures. It feeds my soul and gives me spiritual information to refer to when I need encouragement.

In this way, a journal helps you to enter the presence of God. It feeds you spiritually and enables you to go back to your family and their demands with new insights and strength.

Meditation

■ *What is meditation?*

Meditation helps a person enter the presence of God. For instance, meditation could be referred to as deep prayer. The psalmist refers to prayer as being an incense to God and further states that meditating on the Scriptures brings prosperity (Psalm 1:2-3). Daniel talked of seeking God through prayer and dreams and went to his window every morning and evening to seek God's presence. The book of Acts instructs us to devote ourselves to prayer, especially during difficult times.

Finding and being in the presence of God helps people grow and gain inner strength to deal with their families and their lives. Prayer and meditation make each individual's spiritual journey a personal event.

If you are beginning to think about a spiritual journey but are unfamiliar with the process, you may want to read an account of Christ's life as written in the Gospels of Matthew,

Mark, Luke, and John. If this is too much or you are of another faith, read something that is spiritually inspirational to you. A Jewish person, for instance, may want to read the Psalms, Isaiah, and Proverbs, which are some of my favorites.

FAMILY STORY

Martha spent some time developing her journal writing with Joyce's group and then decided she wanted to learn more about prayer. Joyce informed her that the women's group was having someone come to lead a prayer and meditation the following week. Fifteen women showed up that week, and several chose to read excerpts from their journals, which were moving to Martha. One woman shared how her stepson had been sick that week and she had sat with him in his room. She had been able to get closer to him in that period than he had let her before.

One of the leaders announced that those women who felt comfortable could participate in a guided meditation on experiencing God's love. Those who were interested got into comfortable positions, either sitting or lying on the floor, and were then asked to close their eyes and to visualize a place in their mind that felt safe and comforting. They were then instructed to see God entering that place with them. The women were each asked how they envisioned God. Who in their life that loved them did God remind them of? What did God do in that safe place to help them feel safe and healed? What questions did they have to ask God? What did God say to them? She encouraged them to spend some time silently on their own with God. When they were ready, she asked them to come back to this day, bringing with them what they had learned with those feelings of safety and love.

165

Martha noticed that all the women involved in the guided meditation shared an awareness of the presence of God in their lives and experienced the spiritual side of themselves. They all were painfully honest about their struggles, and some admitted they could not see God as a comforting figure. ■

This example may be foreign and frightening to you if you have never experienced a guided meditation before, but read this section before giving up. Let's explore meditation a little.

■ *Steps in meditation*

Create your own space. As with journal writing, you must find a place where you can be quiet and comfortable for your meditation. This could be your bedroom, den, or any place that feels safe to you where you will not be disturbed. Some people even have a special room for this purpose. It is especially important that your body is comfortable during your time of meditation.

"Be still and know that I am God . . ." (Psalm 46:10). It takes some time to unhook from our busy schedules and focus our minds on what God has to tell us. Our minds race with a thousand thoughts all day long. We must empty our minds of all outside distractions when we come to our "closet" for prayer. This is by no means the same as turning off our minds or giving up our intellect. It helps us focus on God so that we can be aware of the divine presence. A period of silence allows us to enter this time of communion.

Learn to relax. Relaxation is one of the ways in which we can open ourselves to our spiritual side. The stresses of our

Spiritual Journeys

everyday life and the new family take their toll on us physically, as well as emotionally and spiritually. Courses on stress management suggest taking two fifteen-minute periods out of every day for relaxation, meditation, and exercise.

It is important to sit or lie down in a spot that will be comfortable for a period of time. Relaxation tapes and soothing music can also help. Employ whatever methods that will help you relax, and breathe freely and deeply from the diaphragm. Breathe in through the nose and blow out through your mouth, as slowly and deeply as possible. If you find yourself becoming light-headed, you are breathing too fast. Take it more slowly. You are not competing in a contest, and you don't have to rush. Your only thought should be finding a way to comfort and relaxation.

"Let go and let God." You will find that it takes some practice to become comfortable with each of these steps, but in time they will happen simultaneously. This next phrase has been used by many different people talking about meditation. There may be other phrases that better suit you in letting go of things that are bothering you. As I say, "let go and let God," I envision God taking the problems I am struggling with. Sometimes I will open my hands, palms up, in a symbolic motion of letting go. Sometimes if I have trouble concentrating, I will list incidents, problems, or people to give to God. Be as specific as you can, or just say over and over to yourself, "let go."

This will clear your mind of the daily worries and make another deeper connection with God. We are told throughout Scripture that we can give our problems to God. Moses, for example, was always going to God, who provided food, direction, and protection as the people of Israel journeyed toward their new land.

167

Practice being in God's presence. God created us with a spiritual side to our being, so what I'm referring to is the need to connect our spiritual side with God. How do we do this? One way is to ask God directly. When you are in this quiet place of prayer you may want to ask, in some form: "Help me to know you, your presence." Sometimes I imagine a meeting between God and myself. At a time in my life when it was very difficult for me to go to church I experienced an interesting image. When I was in the service, I imagined Christ meeting me on a beach and sitting on the sand to talk with me.

With practice, you may find different ways of relating to God's presence. Don't be discouraged if, at first, you draw a blank. I often say the Lord's Prayer as a way of coming into God's presence. Some people say God's name over and over in one form or another: Jehovah, Jesus, God. Reading, reciting Scripture, or singing a song are some other ways of meditating on God's presence. A feeling of great peace often accompanies this stage of meditation. Some people talk about a certain knowledge of being in God's presence.

At this point, you may want to ask questions or voice prayers for yourself or others. Take the time to hear what is said to you. We often hear prayers in church that are fired off so rapidly we wonder how anyone could have time to hear a response. This is a time to ask for guidance and direction in your life.

Give yourself some time in God's presence and if you don't get an answer right away, don't worry. Sometimes I don't begin to understand the answers to my prayers until I've hit my lowest point or afterwards.

Give yourself some time to come back to your day. Then you can continue with your tasks with more focus and energy.

Pick a time that is best for you. I try to do at least one fifteen-minute period every day, if not two. Several times a week, I try to have a longer time. Once a month, I set aside a half day of retreat to read and pray. Many people suggest getting away for a longer spiritual retreat once a year. Again, I think every person should develop a program that works for his or her special needs.

Use guided imagery. What in the world was Martha doing? What is guided imagery? Guided imagery is just a visual extension of what we have just talked about. It usually involves another person, or a tape, helping you to hear an image described and then visualize it. Sometimes, if we can picture what the thoughts inside of us look like we can see what we are struggling with. We do not always have words for these thoughts, but with some guidance we can get helpful images. There are tapes, books, and workshops on guided imagery. The family story provides an example of how different people got in touch with their various ways of seeing God. Guided imagery can help pinpoint problems and pain in our lives. Martha was helped through guided imagery to see her attitudes more clearly and know where to begin her spiritual journey.

One word of caution, in attending a workshop or in dealing with the subject of meditation: Be sure the people involved believe in the divinity of God. (There are some religious groups and cults whose practices are dangerous or, at the very least, unhealthy.) Don't go anywhere you don't want to go. God is big enough and creative enough to meet you in whatever meditation process works for you. In fact, the type of meditation experience that works for you will have a lot to do with the kind of religious environment you are comfortable with. Some people have no problem in crossing denominational boundaries in order to find the best experience for their spiritual growth; others do not feel safe in doing this. It is pointless to enlist the help of those whose basic beliefs about

God are quite different from yours if this is going to make you feel unsafe or add to your confusion.

Once you have some experience with meditation, it can be shared with others, if that is your choice, and the techniques can be used to bring about healing and forgiveness in your family.

Forgiveness

What does all this have to do with forgiveness? Entering into a deep prayer life can help you forgive the people who have hurt you. I have found in my work with blended families that there is much need for forgiveness. The bonding process takes time, and family members—past and present—can cause pain that, at first, seems unforgivable.

What is forgiveness? We hear, especially in religious circles, that we must forgive, but how is it really achieved? Why is forgiveness important for ourselves and for our families?

■ *What is it?*

Forgiveness could be defined as unconditional love or true empathy. We come to see the person that hurt us as a human being with faults and pain of his own. This pain made him act in a hurtful way toward us. We can come to a place where we forgive him for what he has so wrongfully done to us. It is not that we accept the hurtful behavior, but we empathize with him and can forgive him.

There are several types of what I choose to call false forgiveness. The first type of false forgiveness involves the idea of immediate forgiveness, wherein a person is expected to forget entirely about the incident and never have any negative feelings toward the person who wronged him. Second is a manipulative form of false forgiveness, in which an individual makes a great show of asking another's forgiveness, without any substance to back it up. An example of this is the person who continually neglects or abuses a spouse or a child, then begs for forgiveness with no intention or ability to mend his or her ways. These are often the same people who want you to instantly forgive them after the hurt has been performed.

The purpose of forgiveness is to repair the souls of the people involved and to move beyond the painful experience. I am convinced that, in some ways, the person who forgives gains more than the one being forgiven. Unforgiveness can eat away at our souls to the point of illness. So we forgive to give ourselves peace and to get on with our lives, even if the other person cannot change.

Forgiveness is not a one-shot deal but a daily process that has phases and feelings, not unlike grief. Many times, especially in blended families, the process takes a great deal of time and patience.

Forgiveness is a give-and-take process in the family. As you work on forgiving one member of the family, he or she is working on forgiving you or someone else in the family. This is why it is a good precedent to teach the principles of forgiveness; each member can then understand the importance of forgiveness and work together as a family. It is vitally important, however, not to force any member of the family to forgive before they feel ready. Forcing people only makes their anger worse.

One way to develop a forgiving spirit is to ask God's help during meditation. Without divine intervention, many of us who have experienced so much hurt in our lives could not possibly forgive on our own.

■ *The process*

There are different stages in the forgiving process, but the most important thing is to arrive at a feeling of inner peace and a sense that the wounds have healed. Lewis Smedes, in his book *Forgive & Forget,* points out these important steps:

Whom do you need to forgive?

- Admit there was a wrong done to you and that it hurt you. Allow yourself to feel the pain. Denial of the pain is as much unforgiveness as any other kind of unforgiveness. I had a friend who, if you had done something that you knew hurt him, would say: "No, you didn't; I forgot all about it; Don't give it another thought." This person was swallowing his pain; he was also robbing me of my chance to gain forgiveness. It became increasingly difficult to deal honestly with this friend. Honesty is an important component of forgiveness, first with yourself, and then with others.

- Allow yourself to feel the pain, and to be hurt, upset, depressed, sad, or whatever else it takes to move beyond the situation.

- Explore the incident, and, as best you can, determine what really happened. Give yourself a chance to understand the situation and the circumstances.

What emotions are you experiencing? Rage. As you think about the hurt and feel it, you will also experience anger, which can be full-blown rage at times. Allow yourself to be good and mad at the person who hurt you; this has a cleansing effect on the emotions. It can also give you the energy, if channeled properly, for moving to the next stage of forgiveness.

However, there are those of us who struggle with staying in this stage. This becomes destructive; the human body and mind were not meant to stay in this phase. Our emotions churn, and we strike out at everyone and everthing when we are this angry. If we do not move out of this stage we can become ill in mind, spirit, and body.

Remember the chapter on emotional baggage? If you are stuck in this stage, go back and reread that chapter. The anger has attached itself to some of your unresolved issues, and you need to work them through.

Let go. Where have we seen this stage before? There was a reason for talking about meditation! This is where empathy comes in. We must spend time in prayer and meditation to dissolve the anger, to let go of it, to see the person who has wronged us with the eyes of love, to ask God to help us see the person as God sees us, as forgiven, loved, and cared for.

We must also work on understanding why the person did these hurtful things to us. If we understand that the other person in our family is acting out his pain, we can have empathy for him. In this way, we have forgiven the person. This takes time, and work! It certainly won't happen overnight.

Try to reunite. Ideally, after forgiving the person who has wronged you, it would make sense to try to repair the relationship. Sometimes this is not possible for various reasons:

• It may not be safe to be reunited in the relationship. If a person has been sexually abused or harmed in some other physical way, that individual should ensure his or her own personal safety.

- The person you have gone to will not listen to you or admit wrongdoing.

- The transgressor may be unwilling to refrain from the same or other hurtful behavior.

- The person no longer wants a relationship.

- You may not feel you can have an honest relationship with the person who wronged you.

If it is the case that you cannot reunite, you must console yourself with the thought that you are healing with God's help, and that is all you can do. You must then work on getting on with your life, knowing that you are free.

FAMILY STORY

Martha discovered through her journal writing and prayer that she had buried a lot of hostility toward Steve's oldest son, Sam. Martha and Sam had been at odds almost from the day they met. When Martha asked him to do something, he would react by going in the opposite direction. If she spoke to him, he would fail to respond, or mock her under his breath as he walked away. Attempts to confront him about his behavior met with similar success. They were living in a state of siege with each other, neither talking to the other unless absolutely necessary. This made for a tense situation in the house. What

Martha didn't realize was that she needed to forgive Sam. The situation had become so routine that she didn't see the obvious: she had buried her anger because rage was never acceptable in her family. ■

What indicates that Martha needs to go through the process of forgiveness?

What makes it difficult sometimes for us to be honest with ourselves?

■ *When you need to be forgiven*

Forgive yourself. One of the hardest people to forgive is yourself. I believe one of the reasons for that is the strictness that characterized our families when we were growing up. We were told that we were bad when we didn't behave properly, and we were punished too severely and physically for things that could have been corrected in much healthier ways. As you seek to forgive yourself, it is necessary to realize that you are punishing yourself for something that is not your fault, and absolve yourself by forgiving the true wrongdoers, be they parents, siblings, teachers, or friends. Also, through prayer and meditation, as well as journal writing, you must work on loving yourself. It becomes easier to love and forgive ourselves and others when we become aware of God's unconditional love.

Ask forgiveness from those you wronged. There is wisdom in the phrase: "Confession is good for the soul." To clear our relationship with ourselves, God, and others, we must be very honest. We must confess the areas where we have wronged or hurt someone else. We may want to write down our confessions and present them to God for forgiveness. This clears the way for us to relate more honestly and to be freed from guilt and pain. Then we can literally rip up the confession, signifying our freedom before God and with others. "If we confess our sins, [God] is faithful and just and will forgive our sins and cleanse us" (1 John 1:9).

Nothing teaches our children more than if we confess the wrongs we have committed against them. They learn to practice this with each other and learn the power of forgiveness. We need to go to the people we have wronged and admit our failings and then ask them to share their hurt with us. Listen and do not defend yourself! Then tell them you are sorry for causing them pain and that you will try hard, with God's help, not to repeat the harmful behavior. Then ask them to forgive you. Establish the fact that you want to continue your relationship with them once they feel ready. This is called restoration, the healing of the relationship.

FAMILY STORY

Martha wrote down all the hurts she felt Sam had inflicted on her when it suddenly occurred to her that she had hurt Sam as well. She prayed and asked God to reveal all the mistakes she had made. Again, in her family growing up, parents never asked forgiveness from their children! To her amazement, her list of transgressions was longer than Sam's! She asked God to forgive her and to provide her with the strength to talk to Sam. She discovered in talking to her husband that he also felt somewhat to blame for Sam's pain. They both went and talked to Sam, but it took some weeks to get to the point where the three of them could speak openly with each other. Little by little, as Martha and Steve practiced forgiveness and empathy, Sam began to open up with his pain and hurt. ■

How has forgiveness—or the lack of it— played a part in your personal history, including your family of origin and any families you had before your blended family?

To what specific situations in your blended family can you apply the priniciples of forgiveness?

If these situations involve the children, how can you and your spouse work together toward restoration?

■ *Forgiving God*

Phillip Yancey wrote a book called *Disappointment with God,* in which he dealt with people's anger toward God. Many times we have had bad things happen in our lives and can't understand where God was while they were happening. Why didn't God intervene? We might have prayed diligently and the loved one still died. We may have suffered abuse as a child, and it feels as if God just watched. We look at a world that is out of control and we wonder, where is God? This is not a theological work, and I do not presume to have the answers to all these questions. But I do know from my own experience that all the same principles of forgiveness can be applied to the hurt we feel toward God. We can be angry with God and express our rage and hurt, and we can ask where

God's intervention was when we needed it so badly. It is only through our honesty and anger that we can find peace and a real relationship with God. I think this is also true of people who have lost faith during the process of their families breaking up.

Some would say that this is irreverent and theologically incorrect to feel about or talk to God in this way. Each of us must deal with God according to our own relationship with God. Scripture says that nothing is impossible with God; it is safe to say that God is able to heal and restore us even of our anger at our Creator. The point is, we can talk to God about anything.

We have seen how developing our spiritual journey can help us come together as a family. We have also explored its benefit to each of us individually in giving us the power to forgive ourselves, our families, and sometimes even God. Let us hope and pray and practice bringing our families together in this deeper way. The next section gives you some exercises to help you and your family achieve this goal.

Exercises for Families

■ *Purpose of the exercises*

Each of these exercises has its own purpose. They are designed to help you get in touch with yourself, your family, and God. They are to help you determine what is happening in your life and the lives of the other people in your family. The exercises will help you communicate with each other and enable you to better identify your feelings and develop insights and solutions for yourself and your family.

■ *How to use the exercises*

Each exercise will have its own specific instructions, but there are some suggestions that apply to all the exercises. You may even find some better ways of implementing the exercises for your needs.

1. The first four exercises are especially helpful if used in order: journal writing, deep breathing, meditation, and affirmation.

2. Exercise 5, a feeling check, is probably most effective after journal writing, but it can also be done after the first three exercises or at a completely separate time.

3. Do not force any of these exercises on yourself or members of your family, for they are meant to be done with an open, willing spirit. If forced, they can push people into feelings they are not ready to handle.

    As I was researching this chapter, I came across some of the prayers and literature from my own spiritual direction. I was amazed at how much more I participate in these exercises now than I did even a year ago.

4. Learn to listen to yourself through your journal and prayers, then apply those skills when sharing with others. Approach these exercises for yourself and especially your children with a listening ear rather than a teaching or telling tongue! You are doing these exercises to learn about yourself and the other members of your new family—not to enforce your point of view.

5. Adopt a spirit of praise. Affirm yourself for trying these exercises and praise your family for their input, even when you don't agree with them.

Exercise 1—Journal Writing

Purpose:
To better understand your life and your feelings, give you a daily release for emotions and frustrations, and help you sort and pray through the situations in your new family

Instructions:
Allow yourself at least twenty minutes to write in a quiet, undisturbed place. After you have become accustomed to writing, you may find it helpful to carry your journal around with you and jot things down as they come to mind. This should be in addition to your quiet writing time. Use any kind of notebook that is comfortable for you, and find a private place in which to keep it. Try to write daily, but spontaneously. I sometimes take the afternoon off to write and walk, especially if I am feeling stressed or cannot solve an important dilemma. Write down whatever comes to mind. Try starting off with feelings, events, dreams, hurts, joys, Scripture verses, prayers, and memories.

Questions or thoughts to consider when journal writing:

1. What is your family history? Growing up? Marriages before this one? How did you come into your present family? What were your happiest times? Your lowest times? Why? Who were you closest to, and why? The most estranged from, and why? Who did you have the most conflicts with, and why? Which childhood accomplishments and events have you felt the most proud of? What situations in your life have proved the most painful? How have these events made you into the person you are today? What or who still holds you hostage or who do you have trouble dealing with? Who are you the most like/unlike in your families?

2. How would you define yourself? What are you like? How do you feel about yourself, your mind, your body, your spirit? Go into as much detail as you can, and write whatever occurs to you.

3. What are some of the most important moments in your life? How did you have a part in making those moments happen, or did they just happen to you? What were some of the circumstances surrounding those moments?

4. How do you see God? How would you define your relationship with God? What would you like your relationship with God to be? When you envision God, what does God look like? What person in your life has helped you to come closer to God and know what God is like? How do you talk to God—or do you?

5. Write a spiritual autobiography of your life, and include a time line of all the incidents where you think God has

worked in your life. Describe people who have been spiritually significant to you, and explain why. Record both the positive and negative experiences in your life.

6. If you could write an ideal life for yourself, what would it be like? What kinds of relationships would you have, and why? Where would you live, and why? What would you do for a living? How would that life differ from your life now? What kinds of decisions could you make in your life to make it more consistent with what you would like it to be? (I am not talking about what you think it *should* be, but what you would want it to be.)

7. What are your prayers today? What are your prayers for yourself? For members of your family? For friends? For spiritual guidance? What would you like to ask God?

Realize that when beginning to journal you will probably write a lot more about the past for a while because you have not written before. It's like catching up or building a foundation. Eventually, you may find that you are focusing more on day-to-day feelings and events.

Exercise 2—Deep Breathing and Relaxation

Purpose:
To help you relax, reduce stress, and prepare for your daily routine. Stress management techniques are most effective when breathing exercises, meditation, and creative imagery are used in conjunction with one another.

Instructions:
Sit straight up on a supportive chair, so your spine is straight with your feet flat on the floor in a relaxed position. If you prefer lying down, make sure your spine is straight, your arms spread out by your side, and your legs apart. The most important thing is to be comfortable and keep your body straight so you can breathe deeply. Loosen any restrictive clothing.

1. Place your hand on your lower abdomen, with your thumb centered on your belly button and your hand resting below, on your abdomen. Do not press down, just let it rest there. This is to monitor your breathing at first, so you know you are breathing deeply from your diaphragm, which will relax you.

2. Make sure you are in a quiet environment, where you will not be disturbed. It may help to play some soothing music or listen to a relaxation tape.

3. Try to let everything go out of your mind. If you have distracting thoughts, try to let go of them.

4. Become aware of your body. How are you feeling? Where is the tension in your body? Are you tired, energized, or somewhere in between? Notice these things, but don't try to change them.

5. Close your eyes. Begin breathing deeply. Breathe in through your nose and out through your mouth. Try to feel your abdomen rise and fall under your hand. This may take some practice, but don't force it. Inhale and exhale as slowly as you can. As you inhale, imagine you

are taking in peace and joy and whatever else you need. As you exhale, imagine letting go of all your pressures, worries, and fears. Try to focus on one or two things to take in and to let go of. Practice for five-minute periods at first, then gradually work your way up to a fifteen-minute regimen.

6. Begin to turn your attention back to your present day and time. Open your eyes, look around, sit up slowly, and stretch your arms and legs. You should feel relaxed and energized.

7. After you become accustomed to doing this every day, you will become more aware of your body and its tensions. Deep breathing exercises become so automatic after a while that they can also be done in the car, at work, or walking down the street.

Exercise 3—Meditation

Purpose:
To help you continue the relaxation process, get in touch with your spiritual side, enrich your prayer life, and relate to God in a deeper way.

Instructions:
Again, allow yourself to be in a quiet, undisturbed place for at least twenty minutes. This exercise is most effective when it immediately follows the deep breathing techniques. Have tapes, reading materials, or your journal nearby to help with the process.

1. Breathe deeply or observe a time of silence so you can clear your mind.

2. Begin with a prayer that will bring you into the presence of God.

   After I have done my breathing exercises, I say the Lord's Prayer to help me fix my attention on God's presence. You could say your own prayer, quote a Scripture passage, or say a word or phrase that is meaningful to you. The point is to spend some time entering the presence of God.

3. Let go and let God. You can use any phrase or verse that will help you let go of the things that are troubling you and enable you to ask for divine assistance. Sometimes I will say, "I give you the problem at my job, etc.," going down the list of things I want to let go of. It is important in both of these stages to repeat the words until you feel some sense of peace or satisfaction.

4. Prayer. There are many different ways of praying, but the important thing is to learn what will help you feel God's presence in your life. Discover how you can best communicate with God and feel communicated to by God. Some people write down their petitions; others talk out loud or pray silently. Prayers can be very formal or casual, talking about issues as they come to mind.

5. Creative visualization. Creative visualization is a way of using your imagination to see a problem solved. It can be used in situations other than prayer, but it proves particularly effective during prayer because visual images help you relate to the power of God. The figure of Christ

will be used in these prayers, but you could use other figures that you are comfortable with, such as God, angels, or saints.

Richard Foster, in his book *Celebration of Discipline*, gives some examples of visualized prayer. We have given some examples of our own here, based on the same idea.

- *Christ coming to meet you.* While in this deep state of prayer imagine that you are in a safe place, and Christ is walking up to you. What does he look like? What is he wearing? He has a very caring, loving look on his face. He is very glad to see you. The tone of his voice is deep with love for you. Where would you like him to sit or stand? What would you like to talk to him or ask him about? Pick just one thing to talk about, something that has been troubling you. What do you imagine him saying to you? He is listening to you very intently and hearing what you are saying. He is telling you how much he loves you and how sorry he is for your pain. What else does he say to you? What else do you want to say to him? What is his response? Remember that you are safe, and nothing can harm you in this space. Christ takes your hands and tells you he will be with you forever. He prepares to leave, and you say good-bye, realizing he has given you something very special and he will be with you in your spirit. You thank him for his presence with you today. You come back to this space and time slowly.

- *Healing prayer.* Picture yourself sitting with Christ, in a safe place full of warm sunlight. You are sick either in body or spirit, and you need his healing touch. As you sit next to him, you are aware of his powerful love. You feel a strong warmth begin to penetrate your body and mind. You are able to direct this light or warmth to the area of your being that you feel needs it the most. You breathe deeply and take in Christ's healing love, letting out the pain and sadness you feel. Do this for a period of time. Sit quietly with Christ. What is he telling you? What would you like to say to him? Share with him all of your concerns and requests. In what way does he meet those needs? Imagine him meeting them in the most creative of ways. When you feel ready, thank him for his continued help.

- *Forgiving prayer.* Envision yourself in a safe place. Christ approaches in great love and sits down beside you. You are feeling upset because there is someone in your life you cannot forgive. You have prayed, but to no avail. So, feeling ashamed, you confess your inability to Christ. You describe the person and the situation that have caused you pain. Christ assures you of his love and says he is sorry you were hurt. Imagine him making a place in your heart for the person you cannot forgive and helping you understand that person's own pain. Christ melts away your wound, making it possible for you to forgive. What does the forgiveness feel like? Know that you can take this feeling into your real life and come back into Christ's presence anytime you picture this moment. Thank Christ for the gift of forgiveness and see his love moving with you as you leave this place.

6. Read and meditate on Scripture. Read any other literature that is spiritually helpful to you.

7. Closing meditation. Give thanks or say a prayer to finish your time in God's presence. I thank God and add some praise time or finish with the next exercise of affirmations. Realize that God's presence is with you wherever you go.

Note: This may seem like a long process, but with practice you will be able to complete all these steps in about half an hour.

Exercise 4—Affirmations and Scripture

Purpose:
The purpose of saying affirmations is to reinforce your beliefs and help change your negative thinking while meditating on the Scriptures brings peace of mind. It is helpful to say these affirmations after meditation or during times of stress. Affirmations can also be used within your family to provide help and encouragement.

Instructions:
Each affirmation or Scripture should be repeated either vocally or silently at least three times. Say them slowly and thoughtfully so that you grasp their full meaning. Think of other affirmations you could create that would be specific to your situation and family. Your favorite Scriptures or phrases can also be written and repeated as needed.

Affirmations:
I am a child of God, created in God's image and loved unconditionally by God for who I am.

God has a unique purpose for me on this earth and has created me with special gifts and talents.

I am forgiven by God, and I ask forgiveness of _____ .
or, I am forgiven by God, and I forgive _____ .

I let go and let God work for me in (situation), and I thank God for working things out.

Scriptures:
Psalm 25:16-18:
deals with emotional pain and forgiveness.

Isaiah 45:2-3:
God goes before us to make a way.

Isaiah 53:5:
God takes our pain.

Isaiah 43:1-2:
God is with us.

Other favorite Scriptures of yours.

Exercise 5—Feeling Check

Purpose:
To help you get in touch with your feelings and monitor your feelings.

Instructions:
As you are doing your daily journal writing ask yourself the questions listed below. If something is upsetting you and you can't figure out what, go through this check list. Write the responses in your journal, and see the changes over the course of time. If people in your family are upset or feeling

down, help them with the process. These questions could also be adapted for children.

1. What am I feeling?

2. Where are the feelings coming from?

3 Are there past memories and hurts that contribute to my present feelings?

4. What happened to me in those memories or hurts?

5. What were my responses in those memories or hurts?

6. Was there anyone there at the time who comforted me? Who hurt me?

7. What do I need now?

8. How can I give myself what I need? Ask others to help? Ask God to help?

Exercise 6—Developing Empathy for Others in the Family

Purpose:
To help you see an incident in your family from another person's point of view. To help you understand and feel what other people are experiencing.

Instructions:

Sit in a quiet place and focus yourself for a period of time. Do this creative visualization exercise, and afterwards write down the responses in your journal. Put the questions on tape to make it easier to listen to, and then close your eyes and listen as you play them back.

You could do this as a family exercise, having one person read the questions aloud while the rest of the family sits or lies down on the floor with their eyes closed. Responses could then be shared by the group in oral, written, or illustrated form.

1. Choose an incident of past misunderstanding or conflict between yourself and another family member.

2. Imagine that you are in a safe place.

3. Focus on the other person in the incident, seeing that individual and the incident in as much detail as possible.

4. What is happening to the other person?

5. What do you hear him/her saying?

6. What do you imagine he or she is feeling? Imagine what you would feel if you were in that person's situation.

7. What image comes to mind when you stand next to him or her? What feelings do you get in touch with?

8. What is happening to make that person feel and act the way he or she does?

9. Can you feel his/her pain?

10. What do you think the person needs from you?

11. Check it out with the person. What does he or she say the feelings are?

12. What would you like to give this person?

13. How can you do that?

14. Ask the person's permission to communicate your empathy.

15. Allow yourself to rest, then come back to the present.

16. Journal your feelings.

17. Consider putting what you learned into action, especially numbers 11 through 13.

This is also an excellent forgiveness exercise, but you may have to perform it more than once to get in touch with your feelings.

Exercise 7—Family Mural

Purpose:
To help your family come together and understand what each member needs from the others. This exercise is meant to bring about family discussions.

Instructions:
Get a roll of brown mailing paper and some fat colored markers. Set aside at least 45 minutes when the entire family can work on a project together. Ask family members to pick a topic for family discussion, and make it clear that each person's ideas and input will be needed. Then spread the paper out on the floor and let each person find a space.

1. Pick a topic. Parents may have to present several topics and then take suggestions. The goal of this exercise is not to solve major conflicts but to get people talking.
    Some examples of topics would be: (a) What do you want our new family to look like? (b) What do you need from different people in this family? (c) What in your past family history was of importance to you? (d) What part of that would you like to bring into this family?

2. Put on some soothing, but not boring, background music.

3. Spread the art materials out on the floor, making sure everyone has enough room.

4. Spend at least twenty minutes, not looking at others' drawings or talking, but DRAWING!

5. When finished, go around the room and have each person talk about his or her drawing, telling what is important to them, what they feel about the drawing, etc.

6. Listen carefully and uncritically to each person. Parents may want to make mental notes to implement #7.

7. Ask supportive questions and make empathic statements.

8. Go around the circle again and have each person say something he or she learned about another person in the family.

9. Hang up the mural where the entire family can see it and study it for a while.

10. Thank everyone for a good job.

11. Repeat the project whenever it seems appropriate for your family, and present it as a fun way for family members to get to know each other better.

Exercise 8—Family Meeting

Purpose:
To have a forum to discuss important issues concerning the family, and to help set up a structure of guidelines that each of the members can respect.

Instructions:
You may have to meet, initially, to talk about the structure of the family meeting itself. The entire family should be present, so that you can get input from each person. Try to keep the time frame within an hour to begin with; meet no more than once a week and no less than once a month. The former is desirable, but you may have to meet more often if unresolved issues come up.

1. Anyone in the family can request a meeting, to which all members are invited.

2. Discuss or agree on a topic either beforehand or at the meeting. Some examples: (a) Family guidelines/chores, (b) vacation, (c) major family expense, (d) stealing, (e) physical harm from a family member, (f) major illness, (g) feeling checks, etc. Feeling checks can be an abbreviated version of exercise 5, but remember that this is not an inquisition. Guidelines and feeling checks provide the basis for the family weekly meetings, but many other topics may come up along the way.

3. Have each family member write down or draw what he or she needs or wants from the family. In a feeling check, the focus is on what each member is feeling.

4. Take time to go around to each family member for his or her input. Follow these guidelines: (a) No one is coerced, (b) everyone may speak frankly, (c) everyone is listened to respectfully and without interpretation, and (d) everyone has *equal power.*

5. Have each individual respond verbally—in writing or by illustration, whichever is most comfortable—to the situation and its possible solution. In a feeling check, each person should reveal what he or she needs.

6. Go around the room once more, asking for further input.

7. Come to some resolution. In situations like chores or guidelines, each person has picked what he or she will do. Parents have recommended what they think will work, and everyone has agreed. Some families vote to narrow down the possible choices. Some families draw

straws, or you may write down the strategies of solving the problem for everyone to decide upon. If you cannot come to a solution, arrange to meet again several days later.

For example: "We've narrowed the possible curfew times down to three choices. Everyone think about it for two days and eliminate one that you cannot live with. In between now and then, let's try to settle curfews individually between the child and parent."

8. If the meeting starts to get heated, either stop to discuss the anger or disband the meeting for several days until everyone can calm down. The meeting should not be allowed to be turned into a battleground.

9. Let the dissenters in the group have their say, and honestly state your beliefs without trying to change their minds.

For example, the parent says to the teenager, "You're entitled to your opinion of wanting to come in at midnight on a school night when you are fifteen. I can't agree with it because of your homework, needed rest, and safety. What can we negotiate here?"

10. Once you have come to a resolution, post it where the entire family can see it.

I recommend family meetings each week so that everyone can choose and alternate their own chores. Post the chore and consequence lists in plain view so that everyone can follow through, including parents!

11. Set up a time for the next meeting and stick to it.

One point of clarification: the entire family meets to make family decisions. However, there may be some family members who need more privacy when setting up guidelines for particular incidents. Examples of this might be bedwetting or dating problems. In these cases, try to use the same format with only the appropriate parent and child. Obviously, you wouldn't post the guidelines; you might, however, write them down for you and the child to agree on.

What other exercises can you and your family come up with that would help you communicate better and, best of all, become friends?

Recommended Readings

Family Life

Berstein, Anne C. *Yours, Mine, and Ours.* New York: Charles Scribner's Sons, 1989.

Brazelton, T. Berry. *On Becoming a Family.* New York: A Merloyd Lawrance Book/Delacorte Press, 1981.

_____. *Infants and Mothers.* Rev. Ed., New York: A Merloyd Lawrance Book/ Delcorte Press, 1982.

Faber, Adele, and Elaine Mazlish. *How To Talk So Kids Will Listen and Listen So Kids Will Talk.* New York: Avon Books, 1980.

Ginott, Haim G. *Between Parent and Child.* New York: Avon Books, 1969.

Napier, Augustus Y., and Carl A. Whitaker. *The Family Crucible.* New York, Bantam Books, 1980.

Paris, Erna. *Step Families: Making Them Work.* New York: Avon Books, 1984.

Schaeffer, Edith. *What Is a Family?* New Jersey: Revell, 1975.

Visher, E.B., and J.S. Visher. *How to Win as a Step Family.* New York: Dembner Books, 1982.

Winnicott, D.W. *The Child, the Family, and the Outside World.* London: Penguin Books, 1964.

Child Abuse

Justice, Blair, and Rita Justice. *The Abusing Family.* New York: Human Science Press, 1976.

Couples

Hendrix, Harville. *Getting the Love You Want: A Guide For Couples.* New York: Harper and Row Publishers, 1988.

Co-Dependency

Black, Claudia. *It Will Never Happen to Me.* New York: Ballantine Books, 1987.

Bradshaw, John. *Homecoming: Reclaiming and Championing Your Inner Child.* New York: Bantam Books, 1990.

Wegscheider-Cruse, Sharon. *Choicemaking.* Deerfield Beach, Fla.: Health Communications, Inc., 1985.

Dreams

Kelsey, Morton T., *God, Dreams and Revelation: A Christian Interpretation of Dreams*. Minneapolis, Minn.: Augsburg Publishing House, 1968.

Sanford, John A. *Dreams and Healing: A Succinct and Lively Interpretation of Dreams*. New York: Paulist Press, 1978.

Spiritual Growth

Hudnut, Robert K. *Meeting God in the Darkness*. Ventura, Cal.: Regal Books, 1989.

Hughes, Gerald W. *God of Surprises*. New York: Paulist Press, 1985.

Kelsey, Morton T. *The Hinge, King of Prussia*. Penn.: Religious Publishing Co., 1977.

_____. *The Age of Miracles*. Notre Dame: Ave Maria Press, 1979.

Lewis, C. S. *Mere Christianity*. New York: MacMillan Publishing Co., Inc., 1952.

_____. *The Problem of Pain*. New York: MacMillan Publishing Co., Inc., 1962.

Schaeffer, Francis A. *True Spirituality*. Wheaton, Ill.: Tyndale House Publishers, 1971.

Smedes, Lewis B. *Forgive and Forget: Healing the Hurts We Don't Deserve*. New York: Pocket Books, 1984.

Stapleton, Ruth Carter. *The Experience of Inner Healing*. Waco, Tex.: Word Book Publishers, 1977.

Webber, Robert E. *Evangelicals on the Canterbury Trail: Why Evangelicals Are Attracted to the Liturgical Church*. Wilton, Conn.: Morehouse-Barlow, 1985.

Journal Writing

Kelsey, Morton T. *Adventure Inward: Christian Growth through Personal Journal Writing*. Minneapolis, Minn.: Augsburg Publishing House, 1980.

Shaw, Luci. *Life Path: Personal and Spiritual Growth through Journal Writing*. Portland, Ore.: Multnomah Press, 1991.

Inspiration and Meditation

Black, Claudia. *It's Never Too Late to Have a Happy Childhood*. New York: Ballantine Books, 1989.

Brueggemann, Walter. *Praying the Psalms*. Winona, Minn.: St. Mary's Press, Christian Brothers Publications, 1973.

Foster, Richard. *Celebration of Discipline*. New York: Harper & Row Publishers, 1978.

Huggett, Joyce. *Open to God: Deepening Your Devotional Life*. Downers Grove, Ill.: InterVarsity Press, 1989.

Job, Rueben P., and Norman Shawchuck. *A Guide to Prayer*. Nashville: The Upper Room, 1983.

Kelsey, Morton T. *The Other Side of Silence: A Guide to Christian Meditation*. New York: Paulist Press, 1976.

Osbourne, Cecil. *Prayers and You*. Waco, Tex.: Word Publishers, 1974.

Schmidt, Joseph F. *Praying Our Experiences*. Winona, Minn.: Saint Mary's Press, Christian Brothers Publications, 1986.

St. Augustine. *Confessions*. New York: Penguin, 1961.

Books for Children

Berman, Claire. *"What Am I Doing in a Step-Family?"* New York: Lyle Stuart Book, 1992.

Black, Claudia. *My Dad Loves Me, My Dad Has a Disease*. Denver: MAC Pub., 1979 (alcoholism).

Blume, Judy. *It's Not the End of the World*. New York: Dell Press, 1982.

Hazen, B. *Two Homes to Live In: A Child's View of Divorce*. New York: Human Sciences Press, 1978.

Helmering, D., and William J. Helmering. *I Have Two Families*. Nashville: Abingdon Press, 1981.

McKay, M. *The Divorce Book*. Oakland, Calif.: New Harbinger Publications, 1984.

Ricci, I. *Mom's House, Dad's House: Making Shared Custody Work*. New York: MacMillan Publishing, 1980.

Bibliography

Books

Black, Claudia. *Double Duty, Dual Dynamics within the Chemically Dependent Home.* New York: Ballantine Books, 1990.

Boszormenyi-Nagy, I., and G.M. Spark. *Invisible Loyalties.* New York: Brunner/Mazel, 1984.

Bowlby, J. *Attachment and Loss Volume I: Attachment.* New York: Basic Books, 1969.

_____. *Attachment and Loss Volume II: Separation-Anxiety and Anger.* New York: Basic Books, 1973.

_____. *Attachment and Loss Volume III.* New York: Basic Books, 1980.

Carter, Elizabeth A., and Monica McGoldrick. *The Family Life Cycle: A Framework for Family Therapy.* New York: Gardner Press, Inc., 1960.

Davis, Murray S. *Intimate Relations.* New York: The Free Press, 1973.

Deutsch, Helene. *Neuroses and Character Types: Clinical Psychoanalytic Studies.* London: The Hogarth Press, 1965.

Erikson, Erik H. *Identity Youth and Crisis.* New York: W.W. Norton and Company, 1968.

Flugel, J.C. *The Psycho-Analytic Study of the Family.* London: The Hogarth Press LTD., 1966.

Freud, Anna. *Normality and Pathology in Childhood: Assessments of Development.* Madison, Conn.: International Universities Press, Inc., 1965.

Goldstein, J., A. Freud, and A.J. Solnit. *Before the Best Interests of the Child.* New York: The Free Press, 1979.

Kubler-Ross, Elisabeth. *On Death and Dying.* New York: MacMillan Publishing Company, 1969.

Mahler, Margaret. *On Human Symbiosis and the Vicissitudes of Individuation.* New York: International Universities Press, 1968.

Miller, Alice. Translated by Hildegarde and Hunter Hannum. *Thou Shalt Not Be Aware: Society's Betrayal of the Child.* New York: New American Library, 1984.

Myers, Michael F. *Men and Divorce.* New York: Guilford Press, 1989.

Parkes, Colin Murray. *Bereavement: Studies of Grief in Adult Life.* New York: International Universities Press, Inc., 1972.

Progoff, Ira. *At a Journal Workshop: The Basic Text and Guide for Using the Intensive Journal.* New York: Dialogue House, 1975.

Register, C. *Are Those Kids Yours? American Families with Adopted Children from Other Countries.* New York: The Free Press, 1991.

Rosenbaum, Veryl, and Jean Rosenbaum. *Stepparenting.* Corte Madera, Calif.: Chandler and Sharp Publishers, 1977.

Sack, Steven Mitchell. *The Complete Legal Guide to Marriage, Divorce, Custody and Living Together.* New York: McGraw Hill, 1987.

Tournier, Paul. *The Meaning of Persons.* New York: Harper and Row Publishers, 1957.

Turner, Jeffery S., and Donald B. Helms. *Marriage and Family Traditions and Transitions.* New York: Harcourt Brace Jovanovich Publishers, 1988.

Val, Eduardo R.. F. Moises Gaviria, and Joseph A. Flaherty. *Affective Disorders: Psychopathology and Treatment,* Chapter 4: Grief, Mourning and Affective States. Dr. Jonathan Lewis M.D. Chicago: Year Book Medical Publishers, Inc., 1982.

Visher, E.B., and J.S. Visher. *Old Loyalties, New Ties: Therapeutic Strategies with Step Families.* New York: Brunner/Mazel, 1988.

Wald, Esther. *The Remarried Family: Challenge And Promise.* New York: Family Service Association of America, 1981.

Walsh, Froma. *Normal Family Processes.* New York: The Guilford Press, 1982.

Ware, Ciji. *Sharing Parenthood after Divorce.* New York: Viking Press, 1979.

Winnicott, D.W. *Human Nature.* London: Free Association Press, 1988.

_____. *The Maturational Processes and the Facilitating Environment: Studies in the Theory of Emotional Development.* New York: International Universities Press, Inc., 1965.

Articles

Bowlby, John. "Process of Mourning." *The International Journal of Psychoanalysis and Bulletin of the International Psycho-Analytic Association,* Vol. 42, Part 4-5, pp. 317-340.

Lutz, Patricia. "The Step family: An Adolescent Perspective Family Relations." *Family Relations Journal,* July, 1983, pp. 367-375.

Mahler, Margaret Schoenberger. "Rapprochement Subphase of the Separation-Individuation Process." *Psychoanalytic Quarterly,* Vol 41, 1972, pp. 487-506.

_____. "On Sadness and Grief in Infancy and Childhood: Loss and Restoration of the Symbiotic Love Object." *The Psychoanalytic Study of the Child,* Vol. XVI, 1961, pp. 332-385.

Messer, A.A. "The 'Phaedra Complex'." *Archives of General Psychiatry,* Vol. 21, August, 1969, pp. 213-218.

Pollock, George H. "Mourning and Adaptation." *The International Journal of Psychoanalysis and Bulletin of the International Psycho-Analytic Association,* Vol. 42, Part 4-5, pp. 341-361.

Ransom, J.W., S. Schlesinger, and A. Derdeyn. "A Step-Family in Formation." *American Journal of Orthopsychiatry,* Vol. 49/1, January, 1979.

Rochlin, Gregory. "The Dread of Abandonment: A Contribution to the Etiology of the Loss Complex and to Depression." *The Psychoanalytic Study of the Child,* Vol. XVI, 1961, pp. 451-470.

Scharl, Adele E. "Regression and Restitution in Object Loss: Clinical Observations." *The Psychoanalytic Study of the Child,* Vol. XVI, 1961, pp. 471-480.

Shambaugh, Benjamin. "A Study of Loss Reactions in a Seven-year-old." *The Psychoanalytic Study of the Child,* Vol. XVI, 1961, pp. 510-522.

Visher, E.B., and J.S. Visher. "Children in Step-Families." *Psychiatric Annals,* September, 1982, pp. 832-841.

Wallerstein, Kelly J. "The Effects Of Parental Divorce: Experiences of Children in Early Latency." *American Journal of Orthopsychiatry,* Vol 46/1, January, 1976, pp. 20-23.

Whiteside, M.F., and L.S. Auerbach. " 'Can the Daughter of My Father's New Wife Be My Sister?' Families of Remarriage in Family Therapy." *Journal of Divorce,* Vol. 1(3), Spring, 1978, pp. 271-282.

Manual

Gordon, Robert, and Leon A. Peek. *The Custody Quotient: Research Manual: Development of the C Q Test Effective Parenting.* Dallas: The Willmington Institute.

Unpublished Articles

Goldsmith, Jean Barnett. *The Divorced Family: Who to Include in Therapy?* Unpublished paper.

Goldsmith, Jean Barnett. *Relationships between Former Spouses: Descriptive Findings.* Paper presented at the National Council on Family Relations, Boston, 1979.

Index

Index